The ICSA G

The ICSA Guide to
Document Retention

Andrew C Hamer LLB ACIS

PUBLISHING

Published by ICSA Publishing Ltd
16 Park Crescent
London
W1B 1AH

© ICSA Publishing Ltd 2004

Reprinted 2006, 2007 by ICSA Information & Training Ltd

Typeset in Sabon & ITC Franklin Gothic by
Paul Barrett Book Production, Cambridge

Printed and bound in Great Britain by
TJ International Ltd, Padstow, Cornwall

British Library Cataloguing in Publication Data

A catalogue record for this book is available from the British Library.

ISBN 978-1-86072-226-4

Contents

Preface   VII

Abbreviations   IX

Part I   Retention principles   I

  1   **Introduction**   2

  2   **Retention policies and procedures**   10

  3   **Retention and disposal schedules**   17

  4   **Review and disposal procedures**   24

  5   **Documents as evidence**   29

  6   **Risk assessments and limitation periods**   40

  7   **Data protection**   61

  8   **Storage of records**   76

  9   **Electronic records**   85

  10   **Life of a company**   97

Part II   Guidance on retention periods   101

  11   **Companies Act records**   102

  12   **Share registration and dividends**   112

  13   **Meetings and minutes**   130

  14   **Accounting and tax records**   138

  15   **Employment and pension records**   154

  16   **Health and safety records**   178

  17   **Contracts, sales and insurance**   196

  18   **Property records**   206

  19   **Information management records**   216

  20   **Financial services and money laundering**   224

Appendix A   Arthur Andersen Trial – sequence of events   250

Appendix B   Sources of information   252

Appendix C   Model retention and disposal schedule   260

Appendix D   Examples of certificates   262

Appendix E   Information survey form – records   264

Index   265

Preface

This book provides guidance on the retention and disposal of documents and other records for businesses established in the UK. It is the successor to the ICSA booklet *A Short Guide to Retention of Documents,* published in 1996. The omission of the word 'Short' from the title of the new Guide reflects the fact that it is more comprehensive in its coverage, than its predecessor.

Like its predecessor, the new Guide concentrates mainly on retention requirements that are generic to most businesses, rather than on specific sectoral requirements, although requirements relating to the financial services sector are covered in rather more detail (see **Chapter 20**).

Many of these generic business requirements will also be relevant to other organisations, such as charities, hospital trusts, government and other public sector bodies, although the Guide makes no attempt to cover the specific retention requirements applicable in these areas.

The Guide is set out in two parts.

Part I includes guidance on:

- retention policies;
- retention schedules and procedures;
- review and disposal procedures;
- general factors that influence retention periods and policies such as–
  - risk assessments,
  - limitation periods,
  - the status of documents as evidence, and
  - data protection.
- retention issues when a company or business ceases to exist;
- particular retention issues relating to –
  - paper records,
  - microfilm records, and
  - electronic records.

Part II is divided into separate chapters for each of the main business functions and:

- includes Retention Schedules which make specific recommendations for the retention of business documents based on good commercial practice and, where applicable, legal requirements;
- provides a commentary on those requirements;
- specifies where specific regulatory rules allow records to be held in electronic form.

Users generally need to exercise caution when applying the recommendations in this Guide. Regulatory requirements are liable to change. Accordingly, sources should be checked on occasion to ensure that they have not been amended or repealed. In addition, it should not be assumed that a record does not need to be retained merely because it does not appear in the retention tables. While every attempt has been made to include all the relevant regulatory requirements, it is simply not possible to guarantee that there have been no omissions. Finally, where recommendations for retention are given, whether in addition to or in the absence of regulatory requirements, they should be treated as such. Part I of this Guide includes background materials and explanations which should assist in applying appropriate retention periods. Users should also consider the impact of any specific sectoral requirements before making any final decisions on retention.

Abbreviations

The following abbreviations are used throughout this book:

APR	Annual Percentage Rate
ASA	Advertising Standards Authority
BASDA	Business and Accounting Software Developers Association
BSi	British Standards Institute
CA	Companies Act 1985
CAWR	Control of Asbestos at Work Regulations 1987
CLWR	Control of Lead at Work Regulations 1980
CHIPS	Chemical (Hazard Information and Packaging for Supply) Regulations 2002
COSHH	Control of Substances Hazardous to Health Regulations 1999
CPR	Civil Procedure Rules
DGFT	Director General of Fair Trading
DTI	Department of Trade and Industry
EDM	Electronic Document Management
ERM	Electronic Records Management
FA	Factories Act 1961
FSA	Financial Services Authority
FSMA	Financial Services and Markets Act 2000
HSWA	Health and Safety at Work Act 1974
ICTA 1988	Income and Corporation Taxes Act 1988
IRR	Ionising Radiation Regulations 1985
LA 1980	Limitation Act 1980
OPS (SA)	Occupational Pension Schemes (Scheme Administration) Regulations 1996
PRO	Public Records Office
RIDDOR	Reporting of Injuries, Diseases and Dangerous Occurrences Regulations 1995

RBS(IP)	Retirement Benefit Schemes (Information Powers) Regulations 1995
RMS	Records Management Society
SWR	Special Waste Regulations 1996
TMA	Taxes Management Act 1970
WORM media	Write Once Read Many
VAT Act	Value Added Tax Act 1994

Part I
Retention principles

1 Introduction

1.1 Why not keep everything?

All businesses generate and receive records. Those records provide evidence of its activities, relationships, rights and obligations, and licence to operate. They can also be an important tool for management, providing the raw data for analysing how the business is doing and how it can be improved.

Some records must be kept for periods specified by law, while others may be needed for purely commercial or management purposes. Either way, most records will have a finite useful life and should be discarded or destroyed when they no longer serve any purpose. This is easy to say, but can involve considerable effort. Few of us have the time, or inclination, to review business documents individually to assess whether or not they should be retained. The great temptation is never to throw anything away so that 'we don't get caught out'. This not only keeps us legal, but also helps to avoid the tiresome task of reviewing documents and files.

Unfortunately, this 'safety first' approach has a number of serious drawbacks. The first of these will be particularly galling to those who 'don't want to get caught out' because it can actually be illegal. Under the Data Protection Act, records that contain personal data should not be kept for any longer than is necessary for the purpose for which they were created (see further **Chapter 7**).

As if this is not enough, our 'safety first' approach can also have significant financial consequences. Storage space for files or records will eventually run out unless we cull records that are past their sell-by-date. This is true of both paper- and computer-based records, although probably of greater consequence in the case of paper as they take up more physical space. It is relatively easy to calculate the direct costs of storing paper records by measuring the area those records occupy and multiplying it by the prevailing market price for renting commercial property of that nature in that area. For records held in storage by a commercial provider, the calculation is even easier. Obviously, it will not be possible to eliminate these storage costs altogether, but it may be possible to reduce them, by moving to smaller premises or letting the space previously taken up by surplus records. However, if nothing is ever done, the records may begin to encroach upon the working environment and undermine operational efficiency. Eventually, the business may face a choice between finding new premises to house them or implementing a retention and disposal policy.

It is tempting to think that the issue of cost does not apply where records are stored electronically. Although, electronic records take up a great deal less space, they may require more regular care and attention. Stored data may need to be converted into new formats to keep up with software and technology developments. The records may need to be transferred to new media periodically because the media on which they are stored may not be reliable beyond a certain age.

The third major drawback of the 'safety first' approach is that it becomes increasingly difficult to find anything as the volume of records increases. This is true of both paper and computer systems. We have all experienced occasions when we know that a document exists but simply cannot find it. Obviously, this sort of problem will not always be a direct consequence of our failure to operate a proper retention and disposal policy. However, our failures regarding retention and disposal will make it a great deal more difficult to find the document once it has been mislaid as the number of places where it could be will be that much greater. Ultimately, the time we spend searching for documents could far outweigh the time it would take us to organise our records.

One of the few good things that can be said about a 'safety first' approach is that, when the inevitable crisis occurs, those who have adopted it will normally find (after much searching) that they have retained a copy of this Guide!

1.2 Arthur Andersen

It is possible that some people will be deterred from implementing a retention and disposal policy by the fate of Arthur Andersen, the audit firm which imploded after being found guilty in the US of deliberately obstructing an official government investigation into accounting irregularities at Enron.

The primary focus of the trial was the allegation that Andersen deliberately shredded documents relating to Enron to prevent them from falling into the hands of investigators. Prosecutors alleged that Andersen had done so knowing that the US Securities and Exchange Commission (SEC) had launched an investigation into Enron and that, if it was found to have acted in breach of SEC rules itself, it risked losing its license to audit US listed companies, having been put on probation by the SEC for its involvement in two previous accounting scandals.

Before the trial began, the case appeared open-and-shut. Prosecutors merely had to prove that a single Andersen partner or employee had at least tried to persuade another to destroy documents pertaining to the firm's audits of Enron with the intention of keeping them out of the hands of the SEC. In the end, the jury was unable to reach a unanimous verdict on this element of the charge, convicting Andersen instead on the basis of alterations made to a memo from which Andersen in-house attorney Nancy Temple asked to have her name removed. The memo detailed a disagreement between Andersen's Professional Standards Group and Enron regarding the accounting of third-quarter losses related to special purpose entities as 'non-recurring'. Ms Temple sent a message saying that she and another attorney's name should be removed from the memo so that they could avoid being subpoenaed.

In many ways it was extraordinary that prosecutors were unable to make the charge for shredding documents stick as there seemed to be ample evidence of abuse (see **Appendix A**). It will probably never be totally clear why the jury failed to convict on this count. However, it was suggested after the trial that it had discounted almost all the testimony of former Andersen partner, David Duncan, who had already pleaded guilty to obstruction of justice and testified to that end during the trial. Andersen's legal team sought during the trial to persuade the jurors that Mr Duncan's admissions were not credible, claiming that he had pleaded guilty not because he had committed a crime, but out of fear of prosecution for more serious crimes like accounting fraud.

The Andersen legal team also attempted to show during the trial that the shredding undertaken by Andersen was routine compliance with a policy designed to protect client confidentiality. Although the evidence seemed to suggest that the shredding had taken place under the cloak of routine compliance rather than in routine compliance, this line of argument was only possible because there was a disposal policy in the first place. If it could be shown that the documents had been destroyed in routine compliance with that policy, this would have been an effective defence against the allegations because it would have shown that there was no corrupt intent.

It is worth noting that destruction in routine compliance with such a policy would not be an effective defence against a charge of destroying a document required by law to be kept for a specified period. At the time, there appears to have been no such requirement in the US in respect of the relevant audit papers, although one has subsequently been introduced by the Sarbanes-Oxley Act requiring them to be kept for at least seven years.

The Andersen case highlights not only the dangers of destroying documents that might be relevant to regulatory or criminal investigations but also the potential benefits of adopting and applying disposal policies. Shredding in routine compliance with established policies would have been a defence against the charges. However, even if it is assumed that this is why the jury did not convict Andersen of the shredding charges, it did not save the firm from conviction on other grounds. And yet, if the shredding had never taken place, it is unlikely that Andersen would have been prosecuted on these grounds alone.

In conclusion, it was not the adoption of retention and disposal policies that led to the demise of Arthur Andersen. Indeed, the Andersen case demonstrates that the adoption of retention and disposal policies can help in such circumstances. Instead, the lesson to be learnt from the case is that destroying documents that may be relevant to a regulatory or criminal investigation will never look good and will probably cause investigators to jump to conclusions, which may or may not be false. To avoid the fate of Arthur Andersen, it is preferable to adopt procedures to ensure documents are not destroyed in these circumstances. This can be done as part of the review stage prior to disposal (see **3.6**).

1.3 Where to start from

As with most administrative functions, it is preferable to perform the relatively mundane tasks associated with retention and disposal on a regular basis and to plan ahead. Failure to deal with the build up of records on a preventative basis will invariably lead to a crisis which may be costly and time-consuming to rectify.

Ideally, retention and disposal issues should be taken into account when systems for storing records and files are first established, irrespective of whether they are to be kept in paper, computer or any other form. Policies and procedures drawn up and applied early on in the life of an organisation will help to avoid problems in the future.

More often than not, retention does not become a live issue until much later on in the life of the business. At this stage, records management systems are already well-established and probably difficult to change. The question being asked is often very simple. How long do we need to keep these records? If they are all of the same type the answer may be very simple. However, if they are mixture of different types or the question is being asked more generally, things can start to get a little more complicated. Ultimately, what is needed is a retention policy that sets out the aims and objectives and retention schedules and procedures that tell people exactly what they need to do as well as when and how.

The scope of these policies and procedures will depend on a number of factors, including:

- the nature of the records;
- the purposes for which they need to be kept;
- how they are going to be stored and accessed (during their useful business life and, if they are required to be kept for longer, thereafter);
- the volume of records;
- the size of the organisation and its stage of development.

One of the first stages in the retention process is to identify the documents and records that the business generates and receives, or is likely to generate and receive, and to categorise them according to certain retention criteria. This is often referred to as an information audit or information survey (see **2.3**).

One of the aims of this process will be to compile retention and disposal schedules. It is preferable for these schedules to be compiled along functional lines so that each department, e.g. the finance or sales department, can focus more easily on the requirements that are relevant to them. It may also be necessary to divide records up according to the system that is, or will be, used to store them, e.g. computer-based records may need to be treated differently from paper-based records.

1.4 Documents, records and information

Although we normally associate the word 'document' with something in paper form, it is capable of a much wider meaning. For example, under the Criminal Justice Act 1988, which sets out rules for the admissibility of documents as evidence in criminal trials, a document is defined as 'anything in which information of any description is recorded'. For the purposes of the Act, a document could include any type of information stored in any form and on any media. It could be information in the form of words, numbers, pictures, maps, plans, sounds, musical notes, etc. The information could be printed, embossed, recorded, processed, engraved, or represented digitally. It could be held in paper form, on microfiche or any other microform, on some sort of computer media, etc. It has even been suggested that a cow that has been branded would be a document for these purposes.

In this Guide, the word 'document' should generally be taken to have this wider meaning unless otherwise indicated. Where the contrary is intended, expressions like 'paper documents' or 'in writing' are used. The law still requires certain transactions to be evidenced 'in writing', i.e. in paper form. Common examples include share transfers outside CREST and the making of a will by an individual.

The word 'record' can also have a formal meaning for records management purposes. It is defined in BS ISO 15489:2001 *Records management* as 'information created, received and maintained as evidence and information by an organisation or person, in pursuance of legal obligations or in the transaction of business'. Records, like documents, can be stored in any form. As all records contain information, they will fall within the standard legal definition of a 'document'. However, for records management purposes, 'documents' are not treated as 'records' until they have been 'selected' for retention. This process of selection is important because businesses will generate and receive many documents that never attain the status of a record. Common examples include draft letters printed out for proof reading, junk mail and copies of master records. The selection process does not need to be complicated. A paper document could be 'selected' as a record, for example, by placing it on a formal file. In the case of computer files, though, it might be necessary to freeze the information within the file and to capture it using a special information management system.

A document which has not been actively 'selected' and 'frozen' as a record may still be admissible as evidence in legal proceedings. Its existence will almost certainly need to be disclosed to the other parties to the proceedings during the discovery process.

1.5 Life-cycle of a record

The main phases in the life-cycle of a record are:
- *Capture* – the initial creation or receipt of the record, and its successful incorporation within an established record keeping system environment.
- *Disposition* – initial decisions made on the appropriate retention period for the record and its eventual fate when no longer active (these parameters will usually be set according to retention schedules for records of that type).
- *Appraisal* – the review process for making decisions on records disposal, whether for permanent preservation or destruction.
- *Preservation* – strategies and mechanisms for preservation.
- *Disposal* – the process of preparing records for transfer to permanent archive for permanent preservation, or final deletion/destruction.

1.6 Records management and information management

A records management system seeks to control the creation, distribution, filing, retrieval, storage and disposal of records which are created or received by the organisation. It takes account of the needs of users but also seeks to minimise the cost of providing an effective solution.

A records management system must also enable the information and knowledge contained within an organisation's records to be accessed and shared within the organisation. This function is becoming increasingly important in the so-called 'knowledge economy', and increasingly achievable with the advent of corporate intranets and specialist 'knowledge management' software products. Indeed, records management does not tend to be called records management any more. Instead, 'information management' is the new buzzword. As far as this guide is concerned, the two expressions will normally be interchangeable.

While the main focus of this Guide is on the retention of records as evidence of the policies and activities of the business, records must also be treated as a management resource. Most of the information required to manage a business still comes from within the organisation itself, so those records need to be organised in a sensible and structured manner so that they can be accessed, analysed and utilised. This is an area where information technology (IT) comes to the fore. IT solutions are hard to justify if all they do is replicate manual systems. The heavy investment involved needs to be justified in terms of productivity, new business opportunities, and better use of management resources. Designing systems to achieve these objectives is a science in itself. It may be viewed primarily as an IT project but will also require careful analysis of the needs of the business, both present and future. Such matters are beyond the scope of this Guide. What is important though is that retention type issues are taken into account when such systems are being designed.

1.7 Some basic records management principles

When designing a new records management system or reviewing a current system, the ideal scenario is for all records of the same type, and for which the same retention period applies, to be stored together in date order. Doing so, makes it easier to apply retention policies, particularly where there are large volumes of records. Indeed, this is often the intuitive way of organising records. Most of us apply this principle without thinking of accounting records, e.g. by storing all customer invoices in date order in the same folder rather than in separate customer files.

It requires a little more effort to apply the same principles to areas where the volume of records is not quite so great. The temptation will often be to keep all records relating to a particular activity or project in one folder so that when any question arises on that matter, one can be sure that the information required is in there somewhere. However, if they are paper records, there often comes a point when the file becomes a bulging mass of unorganised documents of varying importance. We have all faced this situation, that moment of realisation that something needs to be done, to separate the wheat from the chaff. However, very often we simply make a mental note and return the file to its drawer. We know where we want to get to. Unfortunately, like the man who is asked for directions, we also know that we wouldn't start from here. What we need to do is train ourselves and others to take records management and retention issues into account right from the start. Otherwise, like our file, things just tend to get messy and inefficient. This Guide will hopefully help those who are lost in a sea of records to get moving in the right direction.

2 Retention policies and procedures

2.1 Introduction

Most of the decisions that need to be made during the life of a record can be determined in advance by adopting retention policies, procedures and schedules so that, once a record has been identified as belonging to a particular category, all actions taken will be in accordance with the policies, procedures and schedules applicable to that category of record.

This chapter looks at:

- the aims and objectives of retention policies and where we might find them (see **2.2**);
- procedures that will need to be defined for the application of those retention policies (see **2.3**);
- how retention policies, schedules, etc should be produced and applied (see **2.4** and **2.5**);
- monitoring and reviewing retention policies and procedures (see **2.6**).

2.2 Retention policies

Policies associated with retention can come in many different guises. They could, for example, form part of:

- an internal control manual;
- a policy and procedures manual;
- a records management policy;
- an information management policy; or
- an information security policy.

In this Guide, the expression 'retention policy' is used to refer to any policy, by whatever name, which deals with issues concerning the retention or disposal of documents, records or information held in any form.

The overall aim of a retention policy should be to:

- ensure that records required to be kept for legal reasons are kept for the appropriate period and in an appropriate manner;

- after a careful assessment of the risks, minimise the retention of other records while ensuring that the information needs of the business are met;
- retain records in a manner appropriate to their purpose throughout their life and specifically –
  - ensure that records which may need to be tendered as evidence in legal proceedings are kept in a manner that ensures that they will be admissible as evidence in those proceedings and given full weight,
  - ensure that records kept for regulatory purposes are kept in a manner suitable for those purposes.
- dispose of records that are no longer needed in an efficient, orderly and appropriate manner;
- ensure that all disposal actions are properly recorded.

The retention policy may also seek to:

- minimise retention and storage costs;
- ensure that records are handled in the most appropriate medium for the task;
- improve the distribution and flow of information within the organisation;
- ensure that an adequate historical archive is maintained where appropriate.

These additional objectives could form part of some wider information or records management strategy. It is highly likely that an organisation which retains records on computers will need to adopt specific policies to ensure the integrity of the records stored on those systems and an information security policy (see **Chapter 9**). Indeed, one of the dangers is that there can be rather too many policies that impact on the issue of retention and that responsibility for applying these policies may be somewhat diffuse within the organisation. Care obviously needs to be taken to ensure that all the separate policy objectives are integrated and properly balanced.

In general, policies should be adopted at the highest level within the organisation and should, at the very least:

- set broad policy objectives;
- specify who is responsible for issuing and revising subsidiary policies, schedules, manuals and procedures to ensure compliance with those objectives; and
- specify responsibility for monitoring compliance.

In practice, it may be necessary to adopt more detailed policies in order to comply with the British Standards Institute's *Code of Practice for Legal Admissibility of Information Stored Electronically*. This requires policies to:

- include information that would normally be specified in retention schedules;
- state, where appropriate, policy regarding the security classification of each information 'type';
- state policy regarding storage media;
- state policy regarding data file formats for each information 'type', data compression techniques and version control;
- define responsibilities for information/records management functions;
- define responsibilities for compliance with the BSI Code itself.

Adopting such detailed policies can, of course, create its own problems, particularly with regard to amendments. Retention schedules may need to be updated on a fairly regular basis and it may be difficult to obtain board approval for every change that is required. Although the BSI Code states that the policy should be reviewed regularly, it might also be preferable for the policy adopted by the board to allow a specified senior manager or board member to make revisions to certain aspects of the policy (e.g. to retention schedules) between these reviews. It is worth noting, that the earlier, BSI Standard on the use of microfilm and micro-fiche records adopted this broad approach (see **8.5**).

In a conglomerate, with many different kinds of business, most of the policy should be common to all parts of the group. However, each business group or division may well have different needs and sector-specific requirements. These can be addressed in the group policy but it is probably best to deal with them in a separate document. Large groups sometimes issue a group policy and require divisions and business groups to adopt policies of their own which are no less stringent than the group policy.

For new businesses, before anyone has considered how records are going to be managed, it is preferable to adopt a simple policy that will inform that process and ensure that retention issues are taken into account when designing records management systems. At this point, the target audience for the policy is usually restricted to those involved in the design of the records management system. Accordingly, it may be premature to include much more than a simple statement of aims and objectives. Those who need to implement these aims and objectives may, of course, need further guidance on how they can be achieved and, in particular, on the relevant regulatory requirements. It may be a good idea at this stage to adopt as a base line the recommended retention periods established in Part II of this Guide. Although this may not embrace all the records that the business may generate in the future, it at least provides a starting point. Decisions about other records can be taken as and when the need arises, based on the principles set out in this Guide.

2.3 Retention and disposal schedules and procedures

As a minimum, retention and disposal schedules and procedures should:
- identify which documents and records should be retained and the minimum retention periods for each type;
- identify procedures for selecting records for retention or disposal and the frequency with which that selection process should take place;
- specify procedures for the disposal of records (and identify records for which special disposal procedures must be followed);
- allocate clear responsibility for implementation.

Depending on the size of the organisation and the nature and volume of records, the procedure manuals may also cover:
- organisational filing and indexing conventions;
- document security classifications/access restrictions;
- general information security procedures;
- procedures for transferring records to storage and permanent archives;
- procedures for the operation of central registries;
- procedures for microfilming, electronic storage, etc;
- review and consultation procedures; and
- general guidelines.

2.4 Project management

In view of the fact that retention policies will need to be adopted at the highest level it is likely that any project to create, review or revise those policies will need to be sponsored by a main board director, partner or senior manager. A project manager will also need to be appointed with a clear mandate. If the project manager is not a senior manager, he or she will need the support of senior management.

The project manager may well be drawn from one of the following and, if not, will probably need to consult these people during the development process:

- records management professional (if there is one);
- group or departmental representatives (users);
- company secretary and/or a member of the legal department
- administration manager;
- IT manager.

Consultation can be performed on a one-to-one basis or through a representative committee established for the purpose. A committee will inevitably prolong the development process but can sometimes help to promote acceptance of the final policies if end-users are properly represented. This is probably of greater significance for larger-scale records management projects that are intended to result in changes to work practices and staffing. For a retention and disposal policy, a committee might stifle what little enthusiasm exists among the participants.

Expert guidance should be sought where necessary, e.g. the auditors should be consulted before amending policies relating to accounting records and external legal advice should be sought where there is a potential legal liability. It may also be necessary to obtain the permission of external bodies, such as the Inland Revenue or Customs & Excise, before pursuing a particular policy.

External records management consultants can be used if there is not sufficient expertise within the organisation. The Records Management Society can provide lists of firms willing to provide such services (see **Appendix B**).

2.5 A proportionate response

There is only one thing worse than not having a retention policy and that is having one that is not properly applied or implemented. Unfortunately, this is often the fate of a retention policy. No matter how lovingly they are crafted, retention and disposal policies are just not sexy. In fact, they are a bit of a bore to most of us. Accordingly, those responsible for drafting policies and procedures must strive to make them easy to understand and apply. The most common failing is probably that the policy is too complex or disproportionate to the needs of the business. Retention is an area where the KISS maxim ('Keep It Simple Stupid') should definitely be kept in mind at all times.

Policies should be appropriate to the size of the organisation, its commercial requirements and the nature and volume of its records. There is very little to be gained from agonizing over the correct treatment for a particular record when the volume of those records is insignificant. In these circumstances a safety first policy should be applied to ensure compliance with legal requirements. Although there can be no compromise for compliance with statutory and legal requirements, policies that concentrate solely on retaining the fewest possible records are unlikely to be cost effective and may adversely affect operational efficiency.

Policies should be designed with end-users in mind. Those responsible for drafting retention policies can easily become immersed in minute details at the expense of clarity. End users find it difficult enough to generate the necessary enthusiasm for retention tasks without having to wade through long, technical and badly drafted guidelines. Policies should therefore reflect the way documents are filed and used within the organisation. For example, if two classes of document with different retention periods are filed together, the longer of the two retention periods should be applied. If this results in unacceptably high storage costs, the filing system may need to be changed. Retention policies should not be allowed to override operational requirements unless the cost savings outweigh any consequent reduction in efficiency or there is an overriding regulatory requirement.

2.6 Applying retention policies

Although it is important to spend time getting the contents of a retention policy/schedule right, that time will be wasted unless it is properly applied throughout the organisation. An individual of sufficient authority should be given overall responsibility for the implementation of the policy to ensure that it is enforced. In all but the smallest organisations, that individual will need to delegate responsibility to local managers. Copies of the policy (or, preferably, the relevant parts of it) should be circulated to all staff who manage records on a day-to-day basis.

Where responsibility for reviewing records (see **4.2**) is delegated to departmental managers, they should be issued with reminders at appropriate times and be required to confirm that they have undertaken any necessary actions (such as disposal or the transfer of records for disposal or archiving).

2.7 Monitoring and review

In large organisations and conglomerates, a central service function, such as the internal audit department, should be used to ensure that retention policies and schedules are being implemented correctly at a local level by monitoring all sites and departments within the organisation.

Policies and procedures will need to be reviewed on a regular basis. Retention schedules, in particular, will need to be reviewed and amended from time to time to ensure that:

- retention periods and disposal actions are still appropriate in the light of experience and current legal requirements;
- newly-created categories of records are added to the schedules;
- records no longer generated are removed from the schedules after disposal action on them is complete; and
- records which are on schedules as needing retention are still in existence.

3 Retention and disposal schedules

3.1 Introduction

This chapter looks at:
- the purpose and contents of retention and disposal schedules (see **3.2**);
- the main factors influencing retention periods (see **3.3–3.5**); and
- surveys which must be carried out prior to compiling or updating retention and disposal schedules (see **3.6**).

3.2 Retention and disposal schedules

Retention and disposal schedules are used to set out detailed retention and disposal rules for each different type of record within the organisation. Although it may require more effort initially, it is advisable to compile a separate schedule for each independent business function or unit that has control over the creation or capture of records. This helps to avoid changes in the practices and rules that apply in one department from impacting on them all. It also makes it a great deal easier for each department to ascertain the rules that they need to apply. It may also be helpful to sub-divide these departmental schedules into categories according to the system that is used to store the relevant records, e.g. computer-based records may need to be treated differently from paper-based records or microfilm.

A retention and disposal schedule should contain all the following elements:
- name of the operational area creating or holding the records described in the schedule;
- schedule reference and version number;
- reference numbers (where applicable) of the records;
- a descriptions of the records;
- retention periods (see **3.3**);
- review and disposal instructions – disposal options could include a transfer to archives, disposal or destruction using one of several methods (see **4.2**);

- date on which the schedule was agreed and by whom;
- date of implementation of the schedule.

An example of a retention and disposal schedule can be found in **Appendix C**.

3.3 The main factors influencing retention periods

Matters that should be considered when compiling a schedule of retention periods include:

- applicable regulatory requirements (see generally Part II);
- specific sectoral requirements (e.g. the requirements of sectoral regulators) (these are not generally addressed in this Guide);
- business needs and commercial value (see below);
- audit requirements (see **Chapter 14**);
- whether the record might be required to prove compliance with a regulatory requirement (see, for example, Retention Schedule 6: Health and safety and medical records);
- whether the record might be needed as evidence in legal proceedings (see **Chapter 5**);
- risks of non-retention (see **Chapter 6**);
- data protection issues (see **Chapter 7**);
- the media for retention (see **Chapter 8**);
- cost of implementing disposal policy (see **Chapter 4**);
- frequency of disposal (see **Chapter 4**);
- methods of disposal (see **Chapter 4**);
- adding a safety margin to ensure that records are not destroyed before time (see **4.2**);
- any exceptional circumstances;
- the historical value of any records.

i Retention schedules

For organisations compiling retention schedules for the first time, the practices of others in the same trade or business can serve as useful guide. The Retention Schedules in Part II of this Guide list the main types of business records and, where applicable, specify the minimum regulatory retention period for records of that type. Where there is no regulatory requirement, a recommended retention period is given together with the reason(s) for that recommendation. A fairly conservative approach has been taken and the recommendations should only be used as a guide. In the light of experience organisations may find that a longer or shorter retention period is more appropriate. If a shorter period is chosen, it must comply with any applicable statutory or regulatory requirements.

ii Regulatory minimum

Regulatory requirements nearly always impose a minimum retention period, rather than a maximum. Accordingly, there will not normally be any reason why a longer period of retention cannot be adopted. Business needs may, for example, dictate a longer retention period. Special care needs to be taken however in relation to records containing personal data because the Data Protection Act 1998 provides that these should not be kept for any longer than is necessary for the purposes for which the personal data was obtained (see **Chapter 7**).

iii Leeway and exceptional circumstances

It is sometimes sensible to add a bit extra to any regulatory retention period as a safety margin. As it is quite common for users to do this themselves, the recommendations in the Retention Schedules in this *Guide* do not generally make any provision for a safety margin. If they did, users who added their own safety margins could find themselves retaining records for a lot longer than necessary. Where a safety margin has been included in any recommendation, this should be apparent from the difference between 'Regulatory retention period' and the 'Recommended retention period' together with the reasons given in the 'Reasons and remarks' column. A certain amount of leeway can be built into retention schedules by phasing disposal actions. However, this does not cover exceptional circumstances. Special procedures will need to be adopted to ensure that records required beyond their normal retention period are not destroyed (see **4.2**).

3.4 Purposes for which records are kept

The purposes for which records are kept will have a major impact on retention periods and the manner in which they are kept. It may be a good idea to indicate in the schedules what these purposes are, if only as broad categories. This information could be kept elsewhere as part of the overall records management system. For example, it could be entered into a database or information management system. Not everyone who needs it will necessarily have access to this information, and it can be helpful to include some information about the relevant category in the retention schedules. The main categories will probably be as follows:

- *Regulatory* – this indicates that there can be no compromise.
- *Audit* – this may dictate that originals need to be kept until the statutory audit has been completed.
- *Evidence* – this may determine how, for example, electronic records must be treated.
- *Business/commercial* – this category would only be used as the default.
- *Archive* – this would be used to indicate that the record will be permanently archived at the end of its useful life.
- *Document of title* – e.g. share certificates.

Certain records will fall under more than one heading. For example, some accounting vouchers may fall under the heading of regulation, audit, and evidence.

The schedule could also specify any special rules as to the media in which the records may or may not be kept. These days, it is particularly important to specify whether original paper copies should be retained after capture on an information management system.

3.5 Business needs and risk assessments

The need to manipulate information and to make it available within the business may influence the way in which records are kept (see **8.2**).

Usage rates are also likely to have a major impact on retention periods where there are no overriding regulatory requirements. Staff are most likely to need to refer to records early on in their life and it is sensible during this initial period to store them close at hand or make them readily available by some other means, e.g. via a computer network or microfiche records. Where more than one department or business unit needs to access the same records, copies are often made by the department that owns the records for use by the others. The volume of duplicated records may justify the adoption of a different records management system, e.g. the creation of a central registry or the capture of the records on a computer system that allows the information to be disseminated more easily.

The number of referrals to records usually diminishes over time until a point is reached where it may no longer be possible to justify storage at operational sites. In large organisations, where the cost of record retention is significant, the number and type of referrals may be analysed and kept under review to establish the most cost-effective and efficient storage solution. However, most organisations have to rely on the practical experience of users who often tend to exaggerate the importance of records by concentrating on the exceptions rather than the rule. This is even more likely where they find it difficult or time-consuming to gain access to records once they have been removed.

The number of referrals will not always be the main factor when determining the appropriate retention period for a record type. A risk assessment should also be carried out regarding the consequences of non-retention. The assessment will need to take into account the possibility that the record might be required to prove compliance with a regulatory requirement or to defend or prosecute legal actions. As far as legal proceedings are concerned, the appropriate limitation period for any potential legal action will normally provide a guide as to the normal retention period. However, the assessment might also need to take into account previous litigation and claims experience, together with the scale of any penalties or compensation awards and the possibility of insuring the risk. Although it will be difficult for a new business to make accurate assessments of these risks, the experience of others in the same field of activity should perhaps be sought. Share registrars are an example of an industry that routinely makes these types of assessment and insures against some of the risks.

3.6 Information surveys

When addressing records management issues, and particularly when compiling retention and disposal schedules, it is important to know what you are dealing with. In order to find out, it will usually be necessary to conduct an information survey or to review and update an existing survey.

The objectives of an information survey will be to collect (or update) information about records held within the organisation and about the effectiveness of existing records management systems and procedures. For the purposes of compiling retention schedules it will be necessary to collect information on some or all of the following:

- what records are held and the activities to which they relate;
- the purpose for which they are held (regulatory, business, evidence, other);
- in what form the records are held and their location;
- records documentation (file lists, indexes, etc);
- volume of records;
- rate of accumulation;
- whether any copies exist of the records and where and how they are held;
- date range of records;
- frequency of use of the records;
- proportion that are active and inactive;
- restrictions on use and access (e.g. security classification);
- physical condition;
- tracking systems for the records;
- current retention and disposal procedures;
- disposal authority;
- any special records management procedures; and
- whether records management procedures have been properly implemented in respect of the records.

Many of the difficulties associated with introducing new records management procedures can be overcome by careful planning of this information survey. Written authority from top management for the survey to be conducted and advanced warning to staff may help to make the survey more effective. A programme of visits to offices may need to be agreed and the objectives of the survey communicated to the staff involved.

The aims and objectives of the survey will be related to the overall objectives of the records management policy or retentions policy and could include:

- development of retention and disposal schedules;
- development of more economical records storage and retrieval; or
- improvement of active records management systems.

Before commencing the survey, relevant information should be gathered. This could include:

- data on the costs of office space, equipment, supplies and staff;
- any maps and plans of buildings, showing furniture and equipment;
- copies of contracts with commercial storage companies, computer bureaux, etc;

- inventory of equipment, including computers and photocopiers;
- organisation charts;
- procedural manuals and forms;
- copies of file lists or databases; and
- copies of previous studies.

There are two main ways of collecting data in an information survey – physical observation and questionnaires. A physical survey will involve visits to operational areas, looking into each item of records storage equipment, asking questions and recording the findings. These should be carefully planned to avoid disruption. Attention should be paid to the methods used to record the results of the survey. Standard survey forms can be designed for this purpose. An example of a survey form for records is shown at **Appendix E**. A separate form may also be needed to record information regarding staff, space and equipment if relevant to the project.

4 Review and disposal procedures

4.1 Introduction

This chapter deals with procedures for the review and disposal of records, including:

- the review process (see **4.2**);
- disposal instructions (see **4.3**);
- sensitivity categories for disposal (see **4.4**);
- methods of disposal generally (see **4.5**); and
- particular issues relating to the disposal of electronic records (see **4.6**).

4.2 Review process

Someone should always review whether the scheduled disposal action should be allowed to proceed. This is a job that cannot really be done by anyone other than the users of the records and their managers. In the vast majority of cases the answer will be that the disposal action should proceed as normal. However, this will not always be the case and the consequences of failing to identify the circumstances where it should not can be costly and hugely embarrassing. Indeed, this is such an important part of the retention and disposal process that guidance should be issued to staff who will be performing the review function.

Those reviewing records for disposal will need to take into account the following:

- Is there any current, pending or threatened litigation for which the record might be required as evidence?
- Is the business the subject of any regulatory investigation? If so, is this record one that may be relevant to that investigation?
- Is the record still being used or does it contain information that is likely to prove useful in the future?
- Is the record worthy of being kept for historical reasons?

- In the case of a contract, is it still in force?
- In the case of accounting documents, do they also relate to subsequent financial years, and has the tax payable for the relevant year been settled?

The need to retain records for any of the above purposes can have a knock-on effect for records held in a series, particularly those held on computer. In practice, it may be necessary to retain the whole series.

To make the task of reviewers easier, it is good practice to identify records that may be needed for the purposes of litigation as soon as the threat arises. This can be done by annotating the record and/or, if it forms part of a series, separating it from the other records in the series.

A record should be kept of documents approved for disposal action. Where they form part of a series, it is not normally necessary to refer to each document or record individually. Sufficient information should, however, be included to identify the records in the series for which approval has been given and to identify any exceptions. The disposal list may need to specify what disposal action should be taken. This will not be necessary where the action required is the default action specified in retention and disposal schedules but will be where no default is specified or a different action (e.g. archiving) is requested. Disposal lists should be signed off (or authorised in some other way) by an appropriate departmental manager.

Where a decision has been made to retain a record beyond its usual retention period, it should normally be added to a special review list, unless a decision to keep it has permanently been made. Records on this special list should be reviewed occasionally (maybe annually) to check whether the special circumstances that gave rise to that decision still apply.

4.3 Disposal instructions

As far as disposal is concerned, retention schedules could contain a number of elements:

- minimum retention period for which the records should be retained before any action is taken;
- an event which triggers action;
- the action to be taken which might include:
  - a requirement for review,

  - transfer to storage,
  - transfer to permanent archive,
  - destruction (including the method of destruction).

Where a minimum retention period of, say, six years is specified, the event that triggers the disposal action could be the last day of the month, quarter, year or financial year. Any record that is older than six years on one of the dates will then be selected for further action. This allows the timing of disposal actions to be planned, programmed and, if necessary, phased throughout the year. Different departments can be set different dates to avoid bottlenecks in any central or external service involved in the disposal process. Where records need to be reviewed before any disposal action, account should be taken of each department's seasonal workload. Finance departments should not, for example, be expected to treat retention issues as their main priority at the year-end no matter how appealing this may be in retention terms.

4.4 Sensitivity categories

Although it is implicit that a record which is to be destroyed is of no commercial value to the organisation, it may, deal with confidential or personal matters or have other security implications, or be commercially sensitive in the hands of a competitor. The method by which records should be destroyed should therefore be addressed in retention policies and schedules.

One way of doing this is to allocate a sensitivity category to each type of record in the retention schedule and to specify in the policy how records in each category should be dealt with. If possible, the sensitivity categories already used to determine who may access records and how they must be stored should be used or adapted for this purpose. The following sensitivity categories and disposal actions are given merely as an example:

i Non-sensitive (no protective marking)

Ordinary rubbish bins can normally be used for public domain material. Non-sensitive records which otherwise would not be made available to the public should perhaps be torn into small pieces and placed in a rubbish bag for collection by an approved disposal firm.

ii Restricted or personal

This type of waste should probably be strip-shredded and placed in paper rubbish sacks for collection by an approved disposal firm.

iii Confidential or commercial in confidence

This type of waste should perhaps be crosscut-shredded and placed in paper rubbish sacks and pulped or burned.

iv Secret and top secret

The most sensitive documents should be crosscut-shredded or disintegrated using a grille size no larger than 6 mm and placed in paper rubbish sacks. The material should then be burned.

4.5 Methods of disposal for paper records

The main methods of disposal are as follows:

- *Ordinary refuse disposal* – This should be used only for small volumes of non-sensitive records. Wherever the volume of paper justifies it, the option of recycling should be considered.
- *Pulping and recycling* – This is plainly the most environmentally friendly option. However, it may not be appropriate for highly sensitive waste unless it is shredded first.
- *Shredding* – The cost of labour is likely to make this method unsuitable for all but the smallest volumes. For highly sensitive documents some types of shredding may not be sufficient and the waste may itself need to be destroyed to ensure that it cannot be pieced back together (this would be far more difficult if a quality cross-cut shredder was used). If shredding is done centrally, consideration may need to be given to the security of records awaiting destruction.
- *Incineration* – Consideration should be given to the environmental and other safety implications. However, some incinerators are available which will provide heat in the office environment.

Specialist commercial firms can be found to pulp, recycle, shred or incinerate paper records. The security of each firm's methods should be fully investigated and guarantees built into any contract.

4.6 Disposal of electronic records

Care needs to be taken to ensure that sensitive data is completely erased from all electronic storage media. For example, deleting a file on a hard disk may only delete the file reference and not the underlying data. With the right tools and knowledge (both of which are in ready supply), it may be possible to reconstruct the file from the disk. Generally speaking, to remove data from a hard disk properly, it is necessary to overwrite the data several times with a series of zeroes. The number of times this must be done will depend on the sensitivity of the data. Naturally, the task takes longer as one increases the number of times it must be performed. Accordingly, IT personnel will not appreciate having to apply the highest standards to non-sensitive data.

Where back-up media is concerned, it will normally be necessary to destroy the media itself to ensure that it is unreadable. Although some back-up media can be re-used, most IT departments will only tend to do so a few times as its reliability may diminish each time it is used. Once it has reached the end of its useful life, the back-up media should therefore be destroyed in accordance with the usual policies.

5   Documents as evidence

5.1 Introduction

This chapter deals with the rules that determine whether documents and records retained for evidential purposes will actually be admissible as evidence in legal proceedings, and document disclosure. It focuses mainly on the legal position in England and Wales. Both Scotland and Northern Ireland have their own legislative provisions which, although similar, occasionally differ to a significant degree. This is particularly true in the case of Scottish law.

Admissibility of documentary evidence may be affected by:

- the requirements to prove the nature and authenticity of the document (see **5.2–5.7**);
- any special requirements (e.g. for stamped documents) (see **5.8**);
- the status of the evidence which the document contains (certain hearsay evidence is not admissible in criminal proceedings but is always admissible in civil proceedings) (see **5.9**).

The rules on the disclosure of documents in connection with civil legal proceedings are summarised at **5.10**.

Practical procedures to ensure that records stored on microfilm or electronically are included in **Chapter 8** (for microfilm records) and **Chapter 9** (for electronic records).

Where a document is retained as potential evidence, the period of retention will often be determined by the limitation period applicable to actions for which it may be relevant, subject to any overriding regulatory retention requirements and the possibility that retention for the full limitation period is disproportionate to the risks (see **Chapter 6**).

5.2 Documentary evidence

In legal proceedings, documents will normally be tendered as evidence of the information that they contain. The contents of the document may themselves be in issue, such as the terms of a contract, or they may be relevant because of the facts they record, such as the results of medical tests or minutes of a meeting. Very often, a document will be given greater weight than oral evidence about the same fact. This is usually because the document will have been produced contemporaneously or nearer the time of the facts it records.

As a general rule, documents must be 'proved' by a witness who can verify the nature and authenticity of the document before they can be tendered as evidence in legal proceedings. Ordinarily, this would require the party seeking to rely on the document to produce the original together with evidence of due execution by the maker or signatories and, if necessary, evidence of proper attestation. Even under the common law, these rules were subject to numerous exceptions which, for example, allowed copies to be tendered if the original was not available and allowed certain presumptions to be made about a document's authenticity. The methods by which documents may now be proved is the subject of significant statutory modification both for:

- proof of contents (including whether a copy or the original is required) for:
  - criminal proceedings (see **5.3**),
  - civil proceedings (see **5.4**),
  - bankers' books (see **5.5**),
  - public documents (see **5.6**),
  - proof of due execution (see **5.7** and **9.5**).

Business documents will nearly always be admissible as evidence in legal proceedings even if they are hearsay (see **5.9**). It will generally not matter what form they take (e.g. whether they are in paper, microfilm or electronic form) or whether they are copies of the originals. However, it may be difficult to provide the necessary authentication unless the records have been properly managed, particularly in the case of copies. This is particularly relevant in the case of electronic records and microfilm records for which it will be necessary to comply with relevant British Standards (see **9.5**).

Despite all the rules that now allow copies of documents to be tendered as evidence, there will be circumstances in which the original will be of much greater evidential value. A copy of a document is, for example, unlikely to be given as much weight as the original where the validity of a signature is at issue.

Where the law requires a transaction to be in writing (e.g. dispositions of land, share transfers, hire purchase agreements and contracts of guarantee), the original should be retained.

5.3 Proof of the contents of documents – criminal proceedings

Section 27 of the Criminal Justice Act 1988 makes specific provision relating to the proof of the contents of a document in criminal proceedings. These rules only apply if the statement to which the document refers would itself be admissible as evidence. In criminal proceedings this will not always be the case if it could be categorised as hearsay, although there are several important exceptions to this rule, including one specifically for business documents (see **5.9**).

Section 27 provides:

'Where a statement contained in a document is admissible as evidence in legal proceedings, it may be proved:

(a) by the production of that document; or

(b) (whether or not that document is still in existence) by the production of a copy of that document, or a material part of it, authenticated in such manner as the court may approve; and it is immaterial for the purposes of this subsection how many removes there are between a copy and the original.'

For the purposes of this section, a 'statement' means any representation of fact, however made, and 'document' includes 'anything in which information of any description is recorded'. This will include any paper document, map, plan, photograph, tape, recording, film, microfilm, fax and computer disk. It could, of course, also include a whole host of other non-conventional sources that contain information.

The Act does not say anything about the method of authentication required. Whilst this undoubtedly gives the court wide discretion, it is not ideal for retention purposes. The common law rule, which it is assumed that the 1988 Act has replaced, was that the person who made the copy, or who had custody of it, had to testify that it was a true copy of the original. To satisfy the requirements of courts in this regard, it will be necessary to comply with relevant best practice codes issued by the BSI.

Similar provision is made in relation to criminal proceedings before magistrates' courts in section 5F of the Magistrates' Courts Act 1980.

5.4 Proof of contents of documents – civil proceedings

The admissibility of documents as evidence in civil proceedings has been addressed in the Civil Evidence Act 1995. The Act, which abolishes the rule against the admission of hearsay evidence in civil proceedings in England and Wales and repeals the onerous requirements of Part I of the Civil Evidence Act 1968, came into force on 31 January 1997.

Sections 8 and 9 of the Civil Evidence Act 1995 provide:

'8.— (1) Where a statement contained in a document is admissible as evidence in civil proceedings, it may be proved:

    (a) by the production of that document; or

    (b) whether or not that document is still in existence, by the production of a copy of that document or of the material part of it;

authenticated in such a manner as the court may approve.

(2) It is immaterial for this purpose how many removes there are between a copy and the original.

9.— (1) A document which is shown to form part of the records of a business or public authority may be received in evidence in civil proceedings without further proof.

(2) A document shall be taken to form part of the records of a business or public authority if there is produced to the court a certificate to that effect signed by an officer of the business or authority to which the records belong.

For this purpose—

    (a) a document purporting to be a certificate signed by an officer of a business or public authority shall be deemed to have been duly given by such an officer and signed by him; and

    (b) a certificate shall be treated as signed by a person if it purports to bear a facsimile of his signature.

(3) The absence of an entry in the records of a business or public authority may be proved in civil proceedings by affidavit of an officer of the business or authority to which the records belong.

(4) In this section—

    'records' means records in whatever form;

    'business' includes any activity regularly carried on over a period of time, whether for profit or not, by any body (whether corporate or not) or by an individual;

'officer' includes any person occupying a responsible position in relation to the relevant activities of the business or public authority or in relation to its records; and

'public authority' includes any public or statutory undertaking, any government department and any person holding office under Her Majesty.

(5) The court may, having regard to the circumstances of the case, direct that all or any of the above provisions of this section do not apply in relation to a particular document or record, or description of documents or records.'

A copy will include a photocopy, a microfiche record or a copy reproduced from a computer or an optical disk. However, it is important to note that while most business documents will be admissible under the new provisions, the court may still not give the same weight to copies of documents in certain circumstances, e.g. where the document tendered is a poor copy of the original or where questions are raised as to whether a signature is genuine.

Under the Civil Procedure Rules (CPR) a party is deemed to admit the authenticity of a document disclosed to him under Part 31 of the Rules (disclosure and inspection of documents) unless he serves notice that he wishes the document to be proved at trial (r 32.19).

5.5 Bankers' books

Given the frequency with which evidence about bank accounts is required, it would be impossible for the original books to be produced on every occasion. The Bankers' Books Evidence Act 1879, s 3 provides that a copy of any entry in a bankers' book is admissible in all legal proceedings as primary evidence of such entry and of all the transactions and accounts recorded by the entry. The conditions set out in ss 3 and 4 of the 1979 Act must be complied with for this rule to apply. These are:

- the book must be one of the ordinary books of the bank;
- the entries must have been made in the ordinary course of business;
- the book must be in the custody or control of the bank;
- the copy must have been examined against the original entry and found to be correct; and

- proof of these matters must be given by an officer of the bank (either orally or by affidavit).

The definition of bankers' books in s 9(2) of the Act has been extended to include records in written form, microfilm, magnetic tape or any other form of mechanical or electronic data retrieval mechanism.

5.6 Public documents

Many documents of a public nature are subject to special statutory provisions which set out certain formalities for proof of them. This is particularly common for public documents that are frequently required as evidence in legal proceedings. A good example is provided in the Companies Act 1985 for records held by the Registrar of Companies. Section 709 of the Act provides that a copy of or extract from any record held by the Registrar, that is certified by the Registrar, 'is in all legal proceedings admissible in evidence as of equal validity with the original and as evidence of any fact stated therein of which direct oral evidence would be admissible'.

5.7 Proof of due execution

As a general rule, the party relying on a document in legal proceedings must prove that it was duly executed. This normally requires proof that it was made and/or signed by the person alleged to be the author and/or signatory and, where the document is not legally valid without attestation, proof of attestation. These formal requirements can often be dispensed with. For example in civil proceedings, a party is deemed to admit the authenticity of a document disclosed to him under Part 31 of the CPR unless he serves formal notice for the document to be proved at trial (CPR r 32.19(1)). Parties can also make formal admissions of due execution in criminal proceedings (Criminal Justice Act 1967, s 10). In addition, various statutes dispense with the need for proof of execution for public documents.

Where the need for proof of execution is not dispensed with, there is a rebuttable presumption at common law that official documents have been properly executed if they appear on their face to have been properly executed. A private document which is more than 20 years old and which comes from proper custody is also presumed to have been duly executed

(Evidence Act 1938, s 4). Proper custody for this purpose is custody which is reasonable and natural in the circumstances and, not necessarily, the best and most proper place. It is also presumed that a document was made on the date which it bears, that any alteration to a deed was made before execution and that a deed was duly sealed.

Where none of these exceptions or presumptions apply, it may be necessary to prove that a document was written or signed by a particular person. The easiest way to do this is for the person in question to give direct evidence that he wrote or signed the document. The validity of a signature may also be proved by the evidence of someone familiar with the person's handwriting or by comparison, normally assisted by a witness able to give expert opinion. Section 8 of the Criminal Procedure Act 1865, which applies to both civil and criminal proceedings, provides that:

> 'Comparison of a disputed writing with any writing proved to the satisfaction of the judge to be genuine shall be permitted to be made by witnesses; and such writings, and the evidence of witnesses respecting the same may be submitted to the court and jury as evidence of the genuineness or otherwise of the writing in dispute.'

The standard of proof required in civil and criminal proceedings follows the usual rules of 'on the balance of probabilities' and 'beyond reasonable doubt' respectively.

It should be noted that it is possible to sign electronic documents using an electronic signature and that documents signed in accordance with certain procedures will be admissible in the UK as evidence in legal proceedings (see **9.8**).

5.8 Stamped documents

In civil proceedings, but not criminal proceedings, a document required by law to be stamped for the purposes of stamp duty (e.g. a stock transfer form) cannot be given in evidence if it has not been duly stamped in accordance with the law in force at the time it was executed. If an instrument of transfer of securities is not properly stamped, the directors should refuse to pass it because 'if the matter came to be considered in a court of law, and it were proved...that the consideration was not properly stated, the transfer would be inadmissible as evidence, and the directors would have no justification for having taken one name off the register and put another on it' (*Maynard v Consolidated Kent Collieries [1903] 2 KB 121 at 130*).

It is normally possible to pay stamp duty retrospectively, although an additional penalty may be payable in such circumstances.

5.9 Hearsay

'Hearsay' can be defined as 'a statement or assertion made otherwise than by a person while giving oral evidence in the proceedings which is tendered as evidence of the matters stated'. The basic common law rule is that such evidence is not admissible in legal proceedings, although the rule is now subject to numerous common law and statutory exceptions. The main justification for excluding hearsay evidence is said to be that it denies the court of any opportunity to judge the credibility of the person who made the statement or assertion. Documentary evidence will often fall within the definition of hearsay if it is tendered as evidence of the facts stated in the document. A classic example is the case of *Myers v DPP [1965] AC 1001, HL*, in which the defendant was alleged to have acquired stolen cars which he then disguised and sold as renovated wrecked cars. As part of their evidence identifying the cars sold, the prosecution called as a witness the employee who was in charge of the records kept by the manufacturers of the stolen cars. The records in question were microfilms of cards filled in by production line workers showing the details of the numbers stamped on the cylinder blocks of the cars on the production line and showed that the numbers of the stolen cars were the same as the numbers on the cars sold by the defendant. On appeal, the House of Lords ruled this evidence inadmissible as hearsay. The cards were assertions by the unidentifiable men who made them that they had entered numbers which they had seen on the cars.

Subsequent statutory reforms in both the civil and criminal arenas would ensure that such evidence would now be admissible in all legal proceedings.

i Civil proceedings

Section 1 of the Civil Evidence Act 1995 provides that evidence shall not be excluded in civil proceedings on the ground that it is hearsay. This general rule is subject to an important pre-condition regarding the competence of the person as a witness at the time he made the statement (s 5). A party seeking to rely on hearsay evidence in civil proceedings should give advance notice of their intentions. Failure to do so will not affect the admissibility of the evidence. However the court may take the failure into account when deciding whether to grant an adjournment to allow a party to respond to the evidence, or when dealing with costs. It may also treat it as a matter affecting the weight given to the evidence. If all parties agree, these procedural rules can be excluded.

Section 4 of the Civil Evidence Act 1995 directs the court, when evaluating the weight of hearsay evidence, to have regard to any circumstances from which inferences can reasonably be drawn as to the reliability or otherwise of the evidence, including whether:

- it would have been reasonable and practicable for the party by whom the evidence was adduced to have produced the maker of the original statement as a witness;
- the original statement was made contemporaneously with the occurrence or existence of the matters stated;
- the evidence involves multiple hearsay;
- any person involved had any motive to conceal or misrepresent matters;
- the original statement was an edited account, or was made in collaboration with another or for a particular purpose;
- the circumstances in which the evidence is adduced as hearsay are such as to suggest an attempt to prevent proper evaluation of its weight.

ii Criminal proceedings

Section 23 of the Criminal Justice Act 1988 generally makes first-hand documentary hearsay admissible in criminal proceedings if certain conditions about the non-availability of the maker are satisfied. A 'document' is defined for these purposes in Sch 2 of the Act as 'anything in which information of any description is recorded'. Section 24 deals specifically with business documents and generally provides that a statement in a document shall be admissible in criminal proceedings as evidence of any fact of which direct oral evidence would be admissible, if the following conditions are satisfied:

- the document was created or received by a person in the course of a trade, business, profession or other occupation, or as the holder of a paid or unpaid office; and

- the information contained in the document was supplied by a person (whether or not the maker of the statement) who had, or may reasonably be supposed to have had, personal knowledge of the matters dealt with.

This rule applies whether the information contained in the document was supplied directly or indirectly but, if it was supplied indirectly, it only applies if each person through whom it was supplied received it:

- in the course of a trade, business, profession or other occupation; or
- as the holder of a paid or unpaid office (s 24(2)).

Such statements shall not be admissible unless:

- one of the requirements of s 23(2) are satisfied; or
- the requirements of s 23(3) are satisfied; or
- the person who made the statement cannot reasonably be expected (having regard to the time which has elapsed since he made the statement and to all the circumstances) to have any recollection of the matters dealt with in the statement.

The requirements of s 23(2) are that:

- the person who made the statement is dead or by reason of his bodily or mental condition unfit to attend as a witness;
- the person who made the statement is outside the United Kingdom and it is not reasonably practicable to secure his attendance; or
- all reasonable steps have been taken to find the person who made the statement, but that he cannot be found.

The requirements of s 23(3), both of which must be satisfied, are that:

- the statement was made to a police officer or some other person charged with the duty of investigating offences or charging offenders; and
- the person who made it does not give oral evidence through fear or because he is kept out of the way.

5.10 Disclosure of documents

i Civil proceedings

Each party in any civil proceedings must make prior disclosure of any documents in his control that may be relevant to the trial. The rules for disclosure are set out in Rule 31 of the Civil Procedure Rules (CPR). Disclosure is performed by stating that the document exists or has existed. Standard disclosure requires a party to disclose:

- the documents on which he relies; and
- the documents which —
  - adversely affect his own case,
  - adversely affect another party's case, or
  - support another party's case, and
- the documents which he is required to disclose by a relevant Practice Direction.

Parties must conduct a reasonable search for documents falling within points 2 and 3 above. Reasonableness in each case will depend on the:

- number of documents involved;
- nature and complexity of the proceedings;
- ease and expense of retrieval of any particular document; and
- significance of any document which is likely to be located during the search.

Any party to whom a document has been disclosed then has a right to inspect that document except where:

- the document is no longer in the control of the party who disclosed it;
- the party disclosing the document has a right or a duty to withhold inspection of it; or
- it would be disproportionate to the issues in the case to permit inspection of documents within a category or class of document disclosed under r 31.6(b).

For the purposes of disclosure, a 'document' means anything in which information of any description is recorded; and a 'copy', in relation to a document, means anything on to which information recorded in the document has been copied, by whatever means and whether directly or indirectly. A party need not disclose more than one copy of a document. However, a copy of a document that contains a modification, obliteration or other marking or feature must be treated as a separate document.

The court may dispense with or limit standard disclosure and the parties may themselves agree in writing to dispense with or to limit the application of the standard disclosure rules.

The duty of disclosure continues until the proceedings are concluded. Accordingly, if documents come to light during the proceedings, they must immediately be disclosed to the other parties (r 31.11).

6 Risk assessments and limitation periods

6.1 Introduction

As a matter of public policy, the law places a time limit on the commencement of legal proceedings for civil actions. This promotes business confidence and stability and, for our purposes, allows a limit to be placed on the retention of records retained for these eventualities. In England and Wales, the relevant limitation periods are specified in the Limitation Act 1980 (LA). The provisions of the Limitation Act are summarised in **6.4** and set out in more detail in **6.5–6.11**.

The Law Commission has made detailed proposals for reform of the Limitation Act, and its proposals are summarised in **6.12**.

In Northern Ireland, the rules on limitation of actions are contained in the Statute of Limitations (Northern Ireland) 1958, the Limitation Act (Northern Ireland) 1964 and the Limitation Amendment (Northern Ireland) Order 1982. As the regime provided for by this legislation is broadly the same as the regime in England and Wales, no further reference is made to it.

However, the rules in Scotland, which differ from that in England and Wales to a significant extent, are summarised in **6.13**.

Although the law does not require anyone to retain a record merely because that record might be useful to them in the defence or prosecution of legal proceedings, it assumes that they will do so. The inability to produce an admissible record may affect the outcome of the proceedings. This does not necessarily mean that every record that might conceivably be useful as evidence in legal proceedings should be retained during the whole of the limitation period. However, decisions of this nature should be taken after making a careful assessment of the risks of non-retention (see **6.2**).

There is not usually a limitation period for criminal prosecutions. Accordingly, it is difficult to specify how long to keep records that might be useful as a defence against criminal prosecution, e.g. for breaches of regulatory requirements (see **6.3**).

Copies of documents can generally be tendered as evidence in both civil and criminal proceedings (see **Chapter 5**). Accordingly, it may be possible to copy or scan paper records which are being retained solely for limitation purposes for storage in electronic form and to destroy the originals. However, this may not always be the best course of action, particularly where the most important evidential item on a document is a signature or seal. Even then, it is possible to make an assessment of the likelihood of this being the reason that the document is required or whether execution could be proved in some other way (see **5.7**).

6.2 Risk assessments for civil actions

There is no law that requires records that may be valuable as evidence to be retained. However, not doing so involves a degree of risk. The inability to produce a vital piece of evidence could result in the loss of the case or the inability to defend or prosecute a case. In law there is a presumption that a person will keep all papers and records which may be of value but will not keep those which have entirely discharged their duty and which are never likely to be required for any purpose. Facts may, of course, also be proved by other means. However the courts may draw inferences from the fact that a party to a dispute has destroyed relevant documentary evidence.

It is not always easy to predict which records will turn out to be that vital piece of evidence and the natural tendency is to keep far more than may ever be necessary. The main problem in this regard will be to identify the important records and to separate them from those that have little or no evidential value. By doing so it is possible to apply different retention periods. This will be particularly relevant for records relating to matters such as contracts and building projects.

Even though a record can be identified as being of potential value as evidence in legal proceedings, it still may not be worth keeping. The cost of retention may simply outweigh the consequences of being unable to produce it. The chances of it being required may be so slim as to make disposal a risk worth taking.

These types of decisions clearly need to be made after a careful assessment of the risks involved. It will, of course, still be necessary to comply with any applicable regulatory requirements. However, assuming that none exist or that these are shorter than the limitation period for any potential civil actions, it is possible to consider destroying records before the relevant limitation periods have expired.

When making these risk assessments, the following factors will probably need to be taken into account:

- cost of retention;
- possibility of proving facts in some other way;
- previous claims and litigation experience;
- contract values and their range;
- maximum compensation or damages that could be awarded;
- typical compensation or damages awards;
- the range of possible awards;
- potential losses arising from an inability to enforce any rights;
- industry standards;
- the possibility of insuring against any losses arising as a result of the proposed policy.

It will probably be necessary to take independent legal advice as part of this process. The views of insurers may also be relevant if the records relate to risks that are already insured. Any decision taken against the advice of independent legal advisers should be taken at the highest level.

6.3 Risk assessments for criminal and regulatory enforcement actions

It will not be easy to decide how long to keep records that might be useful as a defence against criminal prosecution or regulatory enforcement action, e.g. for breaches of health and safety requirements. Generally speaking there is no limitation period for the commencement of such actions. This may give rise to difficulties when deciding how long, for example, to keep health and safety policies and procedures that have been superseded. It will certainly be advisable to make these documents readily available until the next health and safety inspection. They should also be retained if any investigation is still ongoing in relation to a health and safety incident that occurred while they were in force. Thereafter, they may also be useful as evidence in the event of civil actions relating to accidents and personal injuries that occurred while they were in force. This in itself may be sufficient to justify a relatively long retention period.

Where such considerations do not apply, it may be possible to prove compliance in some other way. For example, compliance with Companies

Act requirements to file returns at Companies House can be proved by the fact that the relevant return appears on the company's file held by Companies House. Accordingly, once the return has been entered on the file, there is no need to keep a copy of that return. In this particular case, retained copies of forms would not prove compliance in any case as the requirements of the Act are that forms must be delivered by a certain period, rather than be sent within a certain period. Accordingly, most company secretaries request a receipt from Companies House confirming delivery of the relevant return. Although these receipts offer proof of compliance, they do not need to be retained once the return has been entered on the company's file. Similar practices could be adopted in relation to other regulatory requirements, although the effectiveness of these procedures will depend on the authority's willingness to issue a receipt and the availability of public registers and information. It is worth noting in this regard, that it is usually easier to obtain a receipt from a regulatory authority or government body for returns which can be filed electronically, the receipt being issued in the form of an e-mail.

Certificates and licences which offer proof of compliance with legal requirements should, of course, always be retained. Where they need to be renewed, old certificates and licences should also be retained. It is normally advisable to keep various records relevant to applications for such licences, although it ought to be possible to set some limit on retention for these purposes.

The fate of the former audit firm, Arthur Andersen, provides a graphic example of the consequences of destroying records that might be relevant to criminal and regulatory investigations and it will always be necessary to adopt procedures to try to prevent this from happening. Destruction of records should be postponed at the merest hint or allegation of criminal activity or fraud.

6.4 Limitation periods in England and Wales

A summary of the limitation periods imposed by the Limitation Act 1980 is provided in the table below. These rules apply to England and Wales only, although the rules in Northern Ireland are very similar. A more detailed analysis of the provisions of the Limitation Act 1980 is provided in 6.5–6.10. A summary of the law in Scotland is provided at 6.13.

Limitation periods usually run from the date of the event giving rise to the cause of action. The cause of action is said to have accrued from that date, hence the use of the expression 'accrual of the cause of action' in the table below. There are several circumstances in which time may start running from a later point, e.g. for personal injury. Where this is the case, there can also be a long-stop limitation period which prevents actions being commenced, say, ten years after the original event giving rise to the cause of action. The court is sometimes given discretion to disapply the relevant limitation period.

Several special factors, such as fraud, may also postpone the running of time for limitation purposes. These are summarised at **6.11**.

Table 6.1: Limitation periods in England and Wales

Nature of Action	Starting Point	Length of Period	Long-stop	Discretionary exclusion by court?
Breach of contract (see 6.5)				
Action founded on simple contract (LA, s 5)	Accrual of cause of action.	Six years.	No.	No.
Action on informal loan contracts (LA, s 6)	Date of written demand.	Six years.	No.	No.
Action on a specialty (e.g. a contract executed as a deed) (LA, s 8)	Accrual of cause of action.	Twelve years.	No.	No.
Actions in tort (see 6.6)				
Action founded on tort (LA, s 2)	Accrual of cause of action.	Six years.	No.	No.
Action for personal injuries or death (LA, ss. 11 and 12)	Later of accrual of cause of action or date of knowledge.	Three years.	No.	Yes.

Table 6.1: Limitation periods in England and Wales – continued

Nature of Action	Starting Point	Length of Period	Long-stop	Discretionary exclusion by court?
Action for defamation or malicious prosecution (LA, s 4A)	Accrual of cause of action.	One year.	No.	Yes.
Action for latent damage (in the tort of negligence) (LA, s 14A)	Later of (a) accrual of cause of action or (b) date of knowledge.	Six years. Three years.	Fifteen Years.	No.
Action under the Consumer Protection Act 1987 (LA, s 11A)	Later of accrual of cause of action or date of knowledge.	Three years.	Ten years.	No.
Claims for trust property (see 6.7)				
Action for non-fraudulent breach of trust (LA, s 21(3))	Accrual of cause of action.	Six years.	No.	No.
Action for fraudulent breach of trust, to recover trust property/proceeds from the trustee (LA, s 21(1))		Unlimited.		
Action claiming personal estate of a deceased person (LA, s 22)	Accrual of cause of action (i.e. accrual of right to share in the estate).	Twelve years.	No.	No.

Table 6.1: Limitation periods in England and Wales – continued

Nature of Action	Starting Point	Length of Period	Long-stop	Discretionary exclusion by court?
Actions related to land (see 6.8)				
Action to recover land, proceeds of sale of land, or money secured by a mortgage or charge (LA, ss 15 and 20)	Accrual of cause of action, (i.e. is, dispossession or discontinuance of possession).	Twelve years	No	No
Action to recover rent (LA, s 19)	Accrual of cause of action (that is, the date rent arrears become due).	Six years.	No.	No.
Miscellaneous (see 6.10)				
Action for sum recoverable by statute (LA, s 9).	Accrual of cause of action.	Six years.	No.	No.
Action for contribution (LA, s 10)	Date of judgment or settlement.	Two years.	No.	No.
Action to enforce judgment (LA, s 24)	Date judgment becomes enforceable.	Six years.	No.	No.

6.5 Claims for breach of contract

The time limit for a claim for breach of contract is six years from the date on which the breach occurs (LA 1980, s 5). However, if the contract is made by deed the limitation period is twelve years (LA 1980, s 8).

For loan contracts at common law, unless provision is made for the date of repayment or repayment is made conditional upon an event, the borrower is instantly liable to repay the debt. The creditor's cause of action accrues immediately the loan is made. This common law rule is mitigated by s 6 of the LA 1980 which provides that in such a situation the six-year limitation period runs from the date on which the creditor makes a written demand for repayment.

6.6 Claims founded on tort

i General

The general limitation period for claims in tort (other than a claim for damages for personal injuries) is six years from the date on which the cause of action accrues (LA 1980, s 2). For torts actionable in their own right, the cause of action accrues immediately the tort is committed. For torts actionable only on proof of damage, the cause of action accrues upon the damage occurring. It is not always easy to predict which of these principles will apply.

ii Damages for personal injuries and related claims

The limitation period applicable to any claim in negligence, nuisance or breach of duty which consists of, or includes, a claim for damages for personal injuries is three years from the date on which the cause of action accrues, or if later, three years from the date of knowledge of the person injured (LA 1980, s 11(1), (2)–(4)). The phrase 'breach of duty' covers actions based on a breach of contract.

Section 14(1) of the 1980 Act provides that a person's date of knowledge is the date on which he first had knowledge of the following facts:

- that the injury in question was significant;
- that the injury was attributable in whole or in part to the act or omission which is alleged to constitute negligence, nuisance or breach of duty;
- the identity of the defendant; and
- if it is alleged that the act or omission was that of a person other than the defendant, the identity of that person and the additional facts supporting the bringing of an action against the defendant.

Knowledge that any act or omission did or did not, as a matter of law, involve negligence, nuisance or breach of duty is irrelevant. An injury is significant if the claimant would reasonably have considered it sufficiently serious to justify instituting proceedings against a defendant who did not dispute liability and could satisfy the judgment: LA 1980, s 14(2).

The court may disapply the limitation period described above if it is equitable to do so in all the circumstances of the case (LA 1980, s 33).

The limitation period for a claim for personal injuries under the Law Reform (Miscellaneous Provisions) Act 1934 is three years from (a) the date of the deceased's death, or (b) the date of the personal representative's knowledge, whichever is later (LA 1980, s 11(5)).

The limitation period for a claim under the Fatal Accidents Act 1976 is three years from (a) the date of the deceased's death, or (b) the date of knowledge of the dependant for whose benefit the action is brought, whichever is later (LA 1980, s 12).

In both cases, the facts of which the personal representative must have knowledge are set out in s 14 of the 1980 Act, and the court may disapply the limitation period if it is equitable to do so (LA 1980 s 33).

iii Latent damage (other than personal injury) caused by negligence

The limitation period applicable to any claim in negligence, other than one which includes a claim for personal injuries, is either (a) six years from the date on which the cause of action accrues, or (b) three years from the 'starting date', whichever is later (LA 1980, s 14A(1) and (4)). The 'starting date' is the earliest date on which the claimant first had both the right to bring the action and either actual or constructive knowledge of:

- such facts about the damage as would lead a reasonable person to consider it sufficiently serious to institute proceedings against a defendant who did not dispute liability and who was able to satisfy a judgment;
- that the damage was attributable in whole or in part to the act or omission which is alleged to constitute negligence;
- the identity of the defendant; and
- if it is alleged that the act or omission was that of a person other than the defendant, the identity of that person and the additional facts supporting the bringing of an action against the defendant (LA 1980, s 14A(5)–(8)).

Section 14A(9) of the 1980 Act provides that knowledge that any acts or omissions did or did not, as a matter of law, involve negligence is irrelevant. These provisions are subject to an overriding limitation period of fifteen years from the date on which the negligent act or omission occurred (LA 1980, s 14B).

iv Claims under the Consumer Protection Act 1987

The limitation period applicable to a claim for damages for personal injuries or loss of, or damage to, property under Part I of the Consumer Protection Act 1987 is three years from (a) the date on which the cause of action accrues, or (b) the date of knowledge of the claimant, whichever is later (LA 1980, s 11A(4)). The facts of which the claimant must have actual or constructive knowledge are:

- such facts about the damage as would lead a reasonable person to consider it sufficiently serious to institute proceedings against a defendant who did not dispute liability and who was able to satisfy a judgment;
- that the damage was wholly or partly attributable to the facts and circumstances alleged to constitute the defect; and
- the identity of the defendant (LA 1980, s 14(1A)).

These rules are subject to an overriding limitation period of ten years from the date on which the defective product is supplied by either its manufacturer or by the person who imported it into the European Union (LA 1980, s 11A(3); Consumer Protection Act 1987, ss 2(2) and 4(2)). The court may disapply the primary limitation period if it is equitable to do so, but not the overriding limitation period (LA 1980, s 33(1) and (1A)).

v Claims for defamation and malicious falsehood

The limitation period applicable to a claim for libel, slander, slander of title, slander of goods, or other malicious falsehood, is one year from the date on which the cause of action accrues. The court may disapply this limitation period if it is equitable to do so in all the circumstances of the case (LA 1980, ss 4A and 32A).

vi Conversion

The limitation period applicable to a claim for the conversion of a chattel, and any subsequent conversion of that chattel, is six years from the date of the original conversion (LA 1980, ss 2 and 3(1)). The expiry of the limitation period operates to extinguish the owner's title to the converted property (LA 1980, s 3(2)). However where the original conversion constitutes theft, time does not begin to run until the chattel is purchased in good faith (LA 1980, s 4).

6.7 Claims for trust property

i Claims for breach of trust

Section 21(3) of the Limitation Act 1980 provides that the limitation period for a claim by a beneficiary for trust property is six years from the date on which the right of action accrues. However, s 21(1) states that no limitation period applies to actions:

- for any fraud or fraudulent breach of trust to which the trustee was a party or privy; or
- to recover from the trustee trust property, or the proceeds of trust property, either in the trustee's possession or converted to his use.

ii Claims for the personal estate of a deceased person

The limitation period for any claim to the personal estate of a deceased person is twelve years from when the right to receive the share or interest accrues (LA 1980, s 22(a)). However if the action falls within the breach of trust heading no limitation period applies. The limitation period applicable to a claim to recover arrears of interest for a legacy, or damages for such arrears, is six years from the date on which the interest becomes due (LA 1980, s 22(b)).

6.8 Claims to recover land and related claims

i Claims to recover land

The limitation period applicable to a claim to recover land is twelve years from the date on which the right of action accrues (LA 1980, s 15(1)). The overriding requirement for the right to recover the land to be treated as having accrued, is that the land is in adverse possession. Section 17 of the 1980 Act states that the expiry of the limitation period extinguishes the title of the person entitled to maintain the action to recover land. The effect of this, and the nature of the title thereby passed to the squatter, varies according to whether the land is freehold or leasehold, registered or unregistered.

ii Claims to recover proceeds of the sale of land

The limitation period for a claim to recover the proceeds of the sale of land is twelve years from the date on which the right to receive the money accrues (LA 1980, s 20(1)(b)). The limitation period for an action to recover arrears of interest payable for such proceeds, or to recover damages for such arrears, is six years from the date on which the interest becomes due (LA 1980, s 20(5)).

iii Claims to recover rent

The time limit for a claim to recover arrears of rent, or damages for such arrears, is six years from the date on which the arrears become due (LA 1980, s 19).

6.9 Claims in relation to mortgages and charges

The limitation period for a mortgagor's claim to redeem a mortgage is twelve years from the date on which the mortgagee takes possession of the property (LA 1980, s 16). The limitation period applicable to a claim to recover any principal sum of money secured by a mortgage or other charge on real or personal property is twelve years from the date on which the right to receive the money accrues (LA 1980, s 20(1)(a)). The date on which the right to receive money accrues where the mortgaged property is a future interest is provided for in s 20(3) and (7).

In a claim to recover arrears of interest payable on any sum of money secured by a mortgage or other charge, or to recover damages for such arrears, the time limit is six years from the date on which the interest becomes due (LA 1980, s 20(5)). However s 20(6) provides that, where the property was previously in the possession of a prior mortgagee and an action is brought within one year of the end of that possession, all arrears due from the previous possession are recoverable.

The limitation period for a foreclosure action for mortgaged personal property is twelve years from the date on which the right to foreclose accrues. If the mortgagee is in possession of the mortgaged property after that date, the right to foreclose is treated as accruing when the mortgagee discontinues possession (LA 1980, s 20(2)).

6.10 Other claims

i Judgments and arbitration awards

The limitation period for an action to enforce a judgment is six years from the date on which the judgment becomes enforceable, LA 1980, s 24(1). This does not prevent the execution of a judgment after six years, but bars any fresh claims to enforce that judgment. No arrears of interest for any judgment are recoverable after six years from the date on which the interest becomes due, LA 1980, s 24(2).

The limitation period applicable to a claim to enforce an arbitration award is six years from the date of the defendant's failure to honour the award when called upon to do so (LA 1980, s 7). The provisions of the Limitation Act 1980 apply to arbitral proceedings as they apply to legal proceedings (Arbitration Act 1996, s 13).

ii Claims on a statute

Section 8(1) of the 1980 Act provides that the limitation period for an action on a specialty, of which a statute is an example, is twelve years from the date on which the cause of action accrues. However, s 9(1) of the 1980 Act provides that the limitation period for a claim to recover a 'sum recoverable by virtue of any enactment' is six years from the date on which the cause of action accrues.

The nature of the relief sought determines whether a statutory action is governed by s 8(1) or by s 9(1). Where the claimant seeks non-monetary relief the limitation period is twelve years under s 8(1), but where the claimant seeks a sum of money the limitation period is six years under s 9(1).

iii Application to equitable remedies

Section 36(1) of the 1980 Act provides that the court may apply time limits to claims for equitable relief by analogy with the provisions of the 1980 Act.

6.11 Factors which postpone the running of time

i Claimant under a disability

Where a right of action accrues to a person under a disability, the general rule is that proceedings may be commenced at any time within six years of the date on which the disability ends or the person dies (LA 1980, s 28). A person is under a disability if he is a child or a person who, by reason of mental disorder, is incapable of managing and administering his property and affairs (LA 1980, s 38(2) and (3)).

ii Claim based on fraud

Where a claim is based upon the fraud of the defendant, the limitation period does not begin to run until the claimant discovers the fraud, or could with reasonable diligence discover it (LA 1980, s 32(1)(a)).

iii Deliberate concealment

Where the defendant deliberately conceals a fact relevant to the claimant's right of action, the limitation period does not begin to run until the claimant discovers the concealment, or could with reasonable diligence discover it (LA 1980, s 32(1)(b)). Section 32(2) of the 1980 Act provides that a deliberate commission of a breach of duty in circumstances in which it is unlikely to be discovered for some time amounts to deliberate concealment of the facts involved in that breach of duty.

iv Relief from the consequences of a mistake

Where an action is for relief from the consequences of a mistake, the limitation period does not begin to run until the claimant discovers the mistake, or could with reasonable diligence discover it (LA 1980, s 32(1)(c)). An action is one for relief from the consequences of a mistake where the mistake is an essential ingredient of the cause of action.

v Acknowledgment and part payment

Section 29 of the 1980 Act provides for the fresh accrual of the cause of action where the defendant either acknowledges the title or claim of the claimant, or makes a payment for it. However this section only applies to claims:

- for the recovery of land;
- in relation to mortgages;
- to recover a debt or other liquidated sum; and
- to recover a share or interest in the personal estate of a deceased person.

The limitation period may be repeatedly extended by further acknowledgments or payments. However an acknowledgment or payment cannot revive a right of action already time-barred (LA 1980, s 29(7)).

6.12 Law Commission proposals for reform

The Law Commission has made proposals for reform of the law on the limitation of actions in England and Wales (see Law Commission Report No. 270 'Limitation of Actions'). It has recommended the adoption of a core limitation regime, which would apply to claims for a remedy for a wrong, claims for the enforcement of a right and claims for restitution, as follows:

(1) There should be a primary limitation period of three years starting from the date that the claimant knows, or ought reasonably to know:

    (a) the facts which give rise to the cause of action;

    (b) the identity of the defendant; and

    (c) if the claimant has suffered injury, loss or damage or the defendant has received a benefit, that the injury, loss, damage or benefit was significant.

(2) For the purposes of the definition of the date of knowledge, the injury, loss, damage or benefit will be considered to be significant if:

    (a) the claimant knows the full extent of the injury, loss, or damage suffered by the claimant or benefit obtained by the defendant; or

    (b) if a reasonable person would think that, on the assumption that the defendant does not dispute liability and is able to satisfy a judgment, it is worth making a civil claim.

(3) The courts will not have a discretion to disapply the primary limitation period, except in relation to claims for personal injuries.

(4) There should be a long-stop limitation period of ten years, starting from the date of the accrual of the cause of action or (for

those claims in tort where loss is an essential element of the cause of action, or claims for breach of statutory duty) from the date of the act or omission which gives rise to the cause of action (but for personal injuries claims see below).

(5) During the claimant's minority the primary limitation period should not run. The long-stop limitation period should run during minority, but not so as to bar an action before the claimant reaches the age of twenty-one.

(6) Adult disability (including supervening disability) should suspend the primary limitation period. Adult disability should not affect the long-stop limitation period.

(7) The long-stop limitation period should not run where the defendant has dishonestly concealed relevant facts.

(8) Acknowledgments and part payments should start time running again, but not once the primary or long-stop limitation period has expired.

(9) The parties may agree that the limitation regime we recommend should not apply to disputes between them, or should only apply in modified form. They will not however be able to modify our provisions on concealment, minority or other disability or the application of the long-stop limitation period to claims under the Consumer Protection Act 1987.

The above core regime would apply without any qualification to the following actions:

- tort claims (except for personal injury claims, and conversion claims);
- contract claims (on both simple contracts and specialties);
- restitutionary claims;
- claims for breach of trust and related claims, including claims for the personal estate of a deceased person;
- claims on a judgment or arbitration award; and
- claims on a statute.

The core regime would be modified in its application to claims for personal injury. The court would have a discretion to disapply the primary limitation period, and no long-stop limitation period would apply. However, the protection given to the adult claimant suffering from a disability would not be unlimited. Where the claimant under a disability is in the care of a responsible adult ten years after the later of (a) the act or omission giving rise to the claim and (b) the onset of disability, the primary limitation period would run from the date the responsible adult knew or ought to have known the relevant facts unless the responsible adult is a defendant to the claim. All personal injury claims would be subject to this regime, whether the claim concerned is made in negligence or trespass to the person (including claims for personal injury).

The core regime would also extend, with some qualifications, to the following claims:

- claims under the Law Reform (Miscellaneous Provisions) Act 1934 and the Fatal Accidents Act 1976;
- claims under the Consumer Protection Act 1987;
- conversion;
- claims by a subsequent owner of damaged property;
- claims for a contribution or an indemnity;
- claims in relation to mortgages and charges; and
- claims under the Companies Act 1985 and insolvency proceedings.

Claims to recover land and related claims, though not subject to the core regime, would be subject to a limitation period of the same length as the long-stop limitation period, running from the date on which the cause of action accrues.

Actions against public authorities would not be subject to special (shorter) limitation periods. Where the core regime applies to common law remedies for a cause of action, it would also apply to equitable remedies for that cause of action, but delay could still bar a remedy before the limitation period under the core regime has expired. Subject to a few exceptions, the Law Commission does not propose to alter specific limitation periods laid down in enactments other than the Limitation Act 1980. It has recommended that the core regime should apply to all actions unless excluded by another provision of the proposed Bill (or any other enactment).

In a written answer on 16 July 2002, the Lord Chancellor stated that the Government accepted in principle the Law Commission's recommendations on limitation of actions, subject to further consideration of certain aspects of its report, and will legislate when a suitable opportunity arises.

6.13 Scottish law – prescription and limitation

Scottish law uses both the concept of prescription and limitation. Prescription can be described as a legal presumption of abandonment or satisfaction of the claim. It can have the effect of extinguishing the plaintiff's rights. In contrast, limitation is a denial of an action after a certain time without regard to the subsistence of the claim. Historically, Scottish law had no concept of limitation periods, but a number have now been introduced to mirror limitation provisions enacted for England and Wales.

At present, Scottish law on prescription and limitation is primarily contained in the Prescription and Limitation (Scotland) Act 1973. The regime under this Act and the general law can be summarised as followed:

i Short-negative prescription

The 1973 Act introduced a new five-year short-negative prescription period. Unlike the old short-negative prescription periods, the expiry of this five-year period extinguishes the claimant's claim entirely. Schedule 1 to the Act lists the relevant obligations to which this short-negative prescription period applies. These include obligations:

- arising out of delict (the equivalent of tort);
- arising out of contract;
- to pay rents;
- arising under annuities;
- arising from unjust enrichment;
- under bills of exchange and promissory notes.

Separate provision is made by the 1973 Act for personal injury, defamation, and for damage caused by defective products.

Schedule 2 to the 1973 Act specifies when the five-year period starts to run in certain cases. Where there is a series of transactions between the parties charged on continuing account, time runs from the date on which payment for the goods last supplied, or the services last rendered, becomes due. Where work is to be done or payment made by instalments, time runs from the date when the last instalment was due to be performed or paid, as the case may be. In the case of any other type of obligation falling within Schedule 1, time runs from the date when the obligation becomes enforceable. Subject to the discoverability rule for latent damage, this date is deemed to be the date on which the loss, injury or damage occurred.

Where there is latent damage a discoverability test is applied in relation to short-negative prescription. Section 11(3) of the 1973 Act applies to obligations to make reparation for injury, loss or damage caused by an act, neglect or default. It provides that in such cases time does not run until the creditor knows or could with reasonable diligence discover that such loss, injury, or damage has occurred.

There is no judicial discretion to extend or disapply the short-negative prescription period.

The running of the short-negative prescription period is:

- excluded where the plaintiff refrains from making a claim because of fraud on the part of the defender or his agent, or because of error induced by the words or acts of the defender, or while the original creditor is under legal disability.
- halted either by the bringing of a claim or by the making of part performance which clearly indicates that the obligation still subsists, or by an acknowledgement. The acknowledgement must be 'an unequivocal written admission clearly acknowledging that the obligation still subsists'.

ii Long-negative prescription

The 1973 Act also establishes a long-negative prescription period of 20 years. This applies to nearly all actions that are not subject to the five-year short-negative prescription period including most claims relating to property and actions for contribution between wrongdoers. However, it also applies to actions which are subject to short-negative prescription and acts as a long-stop in cases where time under those rules may still be running. It does so because for the purposes of long-negative prescription, time starts running from the date on which the relevant obligation became enforceable.

In the vast majority of claims in delict (tort) or breach of contract the short-negative prescription will prevent a claim being made before the long-negative prescription period becomes relevant. However, it is possible that where latent damage has occurred the short-negative prescription period might still be running when the long-negative prescription period expires, in which case the long-negative prescription will extinguish the claim, effectively acting as a long-stop.

As with short-negative prescription, no judicial discretion exists to extend or disapply the prescription period.

The long-negative prescription period will be restarted by a part performance and acknowledgement, but is not suspended by fraudulent concealment or the pursuer's disability.

A few types of action are excluded from the operation of the long-negative prescription period, including claims under the Consumer Protection Act 1987 (where the provisions are modelled on those for personal injuries but subject to a special ten-year prescription period as provided by that Act); actions for damages for personal injuries; and actions for defamation.

Some actions (including recovery of stolen property from a thief and claims against trustees for their own fraud) are not capable of being prescribed at all (Sch 3 to the 1973 Act).

iii Personal Injuries

Actions for personal injuries are governed by the amended ss 17 and 18 of the 1973 Act inserted by the Prescription and Limitation (Scotland) Act 1984. These are similar in broad terms to those that apply in English law. The restriction which they create is a limitation period rather than a prescription period.

The limitation period is three years from the date when the injuries are sustained or, if later, from the date when the pursuer first became aware, or it would have been reasonably practicable for the pursuer to become aware, that the injuries were sufficiently serious to justify bringing an action, that they were attributable to an act or omission, and that the defender (or a person for whom he was responsible) was a person to whose act or omission the injuries were attributable.

Where the personal injuries result in death, time runs from the date of the death or, if later, the date when the person bringing the action first knew or could practicably have known the facts mentioned above in relation to s 17.

In both cases time does not run while the pursuer is under legal disability. In addition, s 19A allows the court to override the three-year limitation periods for actions for personal injuries if it considers it just to do so.

iv Defamation

Section 18A of the 1973 Act (inserted by s 12 of the Law Reform (Miscellaneous Provisions) (Scotland) Act 1985) creates a limitation period of three years for actions for defamation. This runs from the date of accrual of the cause of action and is defined by s 18A(4)(b) as being the date when the publication or communication first comes to the notice of the pursuer. The court also has discretion to extend the limitation period if it appears equitable to do so.

v Positive prescription

This form of prescription applies to heritable rights and can be compared to the limitation rules applying in English law for actions to recover land. In Scotland the original positive-prescription period was 40 years, but this has now been reduced to ten.

7 Data protection

This chapter deals mainly with rules that must be taken into account when determining retention policies for records that contain personal data. It summarises the provisions of the Data Protection Act 1998 (the DPA) (see **7.1–7.4**) and, in particular the:

- restrictions in the DPA on the processing or use of personal data without the permission of the individual concerned (see **7.6** and **7.7**);
- requirement of the DPA that personal data must not be kept for longer than is necessary (see **7.8**);
- requirement for personal data to be kept securely (see **7.9**);
- rules governing the use of personal data for certain direct marketing purposes that could impact on retention requirements (see **7.12**).

7.1 Data Protection Act 1998

The Data Protection Act 1998 (The DPA) requires every person who is processing personal data to notify the Information Commissioner unless they are exempt. The notification must include the name and address of the data controller and a general description of the processing of personal data. This information is included in a register of data controllers maintained by the Information Commissioner which individuals can consult to find out what processing of personal data is being carried out by a particular data controller.

Exemptions from the notification requirements may apply for:

- some not-for-profit organisations;
- the processing of personal data for personal, family or household affairs (including recreational purposes);
- data controllers who only process personal data for the mainte-nance of a public register;
- data controllers who only process personal data for any one or all of the following purposes for their own business: staff adminis-tration, advertising, marketing and public relations, accounts.

There is no requirement to notify manual records which come within the scope of the DPA 1998, although these can be notified voluntarily.

7.2 Personal data

For the purposes of the DPA, personal data is defined at s 1(1), as:
> 'data which relate to a living individual who can be identified:
> - from those data, or
> - from those data and other information which is in the possession of, or is likely to come into the possession of, the data controller
>
> and includes any expression of opinion about the individual and any indication of the intentions of the data controller or any other person in respect of the individual'.

'Data' means information which:

- is processed using equipment (e.g. a computer) operating automatically in response to instructions given for that purpose (e.g. a software program);
- is recorded with the intention that it should be so processed;
- is recorded as part (or with the intention that it should form part) of a 'relevant filing system' (see below); or
- forms part of an 'accessible record' as defined in s 68 of the DPA (i.e. certain health records, educational records (local education authority schools and special schools only), local authority housing records and local authority social services records).

A 'relevant filing system' includes any set of information relating to individuals which, although not processed automatically, is structured either by reference to individuals or by reference to criteria relating to individuals in such a way that specific information relating to a particular individual is readily accessible. This could include records held in paper files, rolladex, non-automated microfiche, etc.

The Information Commissioner (the regulator under the DPA) has issued guidance on this and other matters of interpretation under the Act which can be found at http://www.informationcommissioner.gov.uk/.

7.3 Individual rights

The Act gives various rights to individuals in respect of personal data held about them by others. It gives rights:

- of subject access;
- to prevent processing likely to cause damage or distress;
- to prevent processing for the purposes of direct marketing;
- in relation to automated decision-taking;
- to take action for compensation if the individual suffers damage by any contravention of the Act by the data controller;
- to take action to rectify, block, erase or destroy inaccurate data;
- to make a request to the Commissioner for an assessment to be made as to whether any provision of the Act has been contravened.

7.4 Data protection principles

Data controllers are required to comply with the eight Data Protection Principles ('the Principles') set out in the DPA. Unless an exemption applies, the Principles apply to all personal data processed by data controllers. Data controllers must comply with them, irrespective of whether they are required to notify and whether or not they have actually notified.

The eight principles, set out in Part I of Sch 1 of the Act, are as follows:

First principle: Personal data shall be processed fairly and lawfully and, in particular, shall not be processed unless certain conditions are satisfied (see **7.6** and **7.7** below).

Second principle: Personal data shall be obtained only for one or more specified and lawful purposes, and shall not be further processed in any manner incompatible with that purpose or those purposes.

Third principle: Personal data shall be adequate, relevant and not excessive in relation to the purpose or purposes for which they are processed.

Fourth principle: Personal data shall be accurate and, where necessary, kept up-to-date.

Fifth principle: Personal data processed for any purpose or purposes shall not be kept for longer than is necessary for that purpose or those purposes (see **7.8**).

Sixth principle: Personal data shall be processed in accordance with the rights of data subjects under this Act.

Seventh principle: Appropriate technical and organisational measures shall be taken against unauthorised or unlawful processing of personal data and against accidental loss or destruction of, or damage to, personal data (see **7.9**).

Eighth principle: Personal data shall not be transferred to a country or territory outside the European Economic Area, unless that country or territory ensures an adequate level of protection of the rights and freedoms of data subjects in relation to the processing of personal data.

Schedule 2 of the Act provides conditions for the processing of any personal data relevant for the purposes of the First Principle, whilst Sch 3 provides conditions for the processing of sensitive personal data relevant for the purposes of the First Principle over and above those set out in Sch 2. Additional Sch 3 conditions are set out in The Data Protection (Processing of Sensitive Personal Data) Order 2000 (SI/2000/417) (the 'Sensitive Data Order').

7.5 Enforcement notices and offences

The Information Commissioner can serve an enforcement notice upon a data controller who has contravened or is contravening any of the Data Protection Principles (DPA, s 40). The enforcement notice may require the data controller to take, or to refrain from taking, specified steps or to refrain from processing any personal data (or personal data of a specified description) altogether, or from processing for a specified purpose or in a specified manner.

If an appeal is lodged the notice need not be complied with pending the determination or withdrawal of the appeal. However, if there are special circumstances that mean a notice should be complied with as a matter of urgency, the Commissioner may include a statement to this effect in the notice together with reasons. The requirement to comply with the notice will not then be suspended if an appeal is lodged against the notice. However a data controller must be given at least seven days from the date of service in which to comply.

The DPA establishes the following offences:

- processing without notification (s 21(1));
- failure to notify the Commissioner of changes to the notification register entry (s 21(2));
- processing before expiry of assessable processing time limits or receipt of assessable processing notice within such time (s 22(6));

- failure to comply with a written request for particulars (s 24);
- failure to comply with an enforcement notice/information notice/special information notice (s 47(1));
- knowingly or recklessly making a false statement in compliance with an information notice or special information notice (s 47(2));
- intentional obstruction of, or failure to give reasonable assistance in, execution of a warrant (Sch 9, para 12);
- unlawful obtaining or disclosure of personal data (s 55(1));
- unlawful selling of personal data (ss 55(4) and (5));
- unlawfully requiring a person to supply a relevant record (e.g. records of cautions, criminal convictions and certain social security records) in connection with their recruitment as an employee; their continued employment; any contract for the provision of services to them; or as a condition of providing goods, facilities or services (for payment or not) which are provided to the public or a section of the public (s 56).

7.6 First Principle: Conditions for processing

The First Data Protection Principle provides that personal data shall not be processed unless:

- at least one of the conditions in Sch 2 is met (except where a relevant exemption applies); and
- in the case of sensitive personal data, at least one of the conditions in Sch 3 is also met (see **7.7** below).

The conditions in Sch 2 of the DPA are as follows:-

- The data subject has given his consent to the processing.
- The processing is necessary for the:
    - performance of a contract to which the data subject is a party; or
    - taking of steps at the request of the data subject with a view to entering into a contract.
- The processing is necessary to comply with any legal obligation to which the data controller is subject, other than an obligation imposed by contract.
- The processing is necessary to protect the vital interests of the data subject.
- The processing is necessary for the:
    - administration of justice;

- exercise of any functions conferred by or under any enactment;
- exercise of any functions of the Crown, a Minister of the Crown or a government department;
- exercise of any other functions of a public nature exercised in the public interest.
- The processing is necessary for the purposes of legitimate interests pursued by the data controller or by the third party or parties to whom the data are disclosed, except where the processing is unwarranted in any particular case because of prejudice to the rights and freedoms or legitimate interests of the data subject.

7.7 Sensitive Personal Data

The Act defines categories of sensitive personal data, namely, personal data consisting of information as to:
- the racial or ethnic origin of the data subject;
- his political opinions;
- his religious beliefs or other beliefs of a similar nature;
- whether he is a member of a trade union (within the meaning of the Trade Union and Labour Relations (Consolidation) Act 1992);
- his physical or mental health or condition;
- his sexual life;
- the commission or alleged commission by him of any offence; or
- any proceedings for any offence committed or alleged to have been committed by him, the disposal of such proceedings or the sentence of any court in such proceedings.

At least one of the following conditions of Sch 3 must be satisfied, in addition to at least one of the conditions for processing in Sch 2 (which apply to the processing of all personal data), before processing of sensitive personal data can comply with the First Principle:
- The data subject has given his explicit consent to the processing of the personal data.
- The processing is necessary for the purposes of exercising or performing any right or obligation which is conferred or imposed by law on the data controller in connection with employment.
- The processing is necessary to protect the vital interests of:
  - the data subject or another person, in a case where consent cannot be given by or on behalf of the data subject, or the data

controller cannot reasonably be expected to obtain the consent of the data subject, or

- another person, in a case where consent by or on behalf of the data subject has been unreasonably withheld.

- The processing:
  - is carried out in the course of its legitimate activities by any body or association which exists for political, philosophical, religious or trade union purposes and which is not established or conducted for profit,
  - is carried out with appropriate safeguards for the rights and freedoms of data subjects,
  - relates only to individuals who are either members of the body or association or who have regular contact with it in connection with its purposes, and
  - does not involve disclosure of the personal data to a third party without the consent of the data subject.

- The information contained in the personal data has been made public as a result of steps deliberately taken by the data subject.

- The processing is —
  - necessary for the purpose of, or in connection with, any legal proceedings (including prospective legal proceedings),
  - necessary for the purpose of obtaining legal advice, or
  - otherwise necessary for the purposes of establishing, exercising or defending legal rights.

- The processing is necessary for the:
  - administration of justice,
  - exercise of any functions conferred by or under any enactment, or
  - exercise of any functions of the Crown, a Minister of the Crown or a government department.

- The processing is necessary for medical purposes (including the purposes of preventative medicine, medical diagnosis, medical research, the provision of care and treatment and the management of healthcare services) and is undertaken by a:
  - health professional (as defined in section 69 of the Act), or
  - person who owes a duty of confidentiality which is equivalent to that which would arise if that person were a health professional.

- The processing is:
  - of sensitive personal data consisting of information as to racial or ethnic origin,
  - necessary for the purpose of identifying or keeping under review the existence or absence of equality of opportunity or treatment between persons of different racial or ethnic origins, with a view to enabling such equality to be promoted or maintained, and
  - carried out with appropriate safeguards for the rights and freedoms of data subjects. The Secretary of State may specify by order circumstances in which such processing is, or is not, to be taken as carried out with appropriate safeguards for the rights and freedoms of data subjects.
- The personal data are processed in circumstances specified by order made by the Secretary of State. Currently the only such order is the Sensitive Data Order. This includes detailed provisions for:
  - processing that is in the substantial public interest and is necessary for the prevention or detection of any unlawful act and must necessarily be carried out without the explicit consent of the data subject being sought so as not to prejudice those purposes, or
  - processing that is in the substantial public interest and is necessary for the discharge of any function which is designed for protecting members of the public against dishonesty, malpractice, or other seriously improper conduct by, or the unfitness of incompetence of, any person, or mismanagement in the administration of, or failure in services provided by, any body or association, and must necessarily be carried out without the explicit consent of the data subject being sought so as not to prejudice the discharge of that function, or
  - the disclosure of personal data that is:
    - (i) in the public interest, and
    - (ii) is in connection with the commission by any person of any unlawful act (whether alleged or established), or dishonesty, malpractice, or other seriously improper conduct by, or the unfitness or incompetence of, any person (whether alleged or established), or mismanagement in the administration of, or failures in the services provided by, any body or association (whether alleged or established),

    (iii) is for the special purposes as defined in s 3 of the Act, and

    (iv) is made with a view to the publication of those data by any person and the data controller reasonably believes that such publication would be in the public interest.

- processing that is:

    (i) in the substantial public interest,

    (ii) necessary for the discharge of any function which is designed for the provision of confidential counselling, advice, support or any other service, and

    (iii) carried out without the explicit consent of the data subject because the processing: is necessary in a case where consent cannot be given by the data subject, or is necessary in a case where the data controller cannot reasonably be expected to obtain the explicit consent, or must necessarily be carried out without the explicit consent of the data subject being sought so as not to prejudice the provision of that counselling, support, advice or other service.

- processing that:
  - is necessary for the purpose of carrying on an insurance business; or making determinations in connection with eligibility for, and benefits payable under, an occupational pension scheme,
  - is of sensitive personal data relating to the physical or mental health or condition of the data subject who is the parent, grandparent, great grandparent or sibling of the insured person or member of the scheme,
  - necessary in a case where the data controller cannot reasonably be expected to obtain the explicit consent of the data subject and the data controller is not aware of the data subject withholding his consent, and
  - does not support measures or decisions with respect to the data subject.

- processing of sensitive personal data in relation to any particular data subject that is subject to processing already under way immediately before 1 March 2000 and where the processing is necessary for carrying on insurance business or establishing or administering an occupational pension scheme, where such processing:
  - is either necessary in a case where the data controller cannot reasonably be expected to obtain the explicit consent of the data

subject and the data subject has not informed the data controller that he does not so consent, or
  – must necessarily be carried out even without the data subject's explicit consent so as not to prejudice those purposes.
- processing of sensitive personal data consisting of information as to religious beliefs (or other beliefs of similar nature) or physical or mental health or condition where:
  – the processing is necessary for identifying or keeping under review the existence or absence of equality of opportunity or treatment between persons with a view to enabling such equality to be promoted or maintained, and
  – it does not support measures or decisions relating to a data subject otherwise than with the data subject's explicit consent, and
  – it does not cause nor is likely to cause substantial damage or distress to the data subject or any other person.
- processing of personal data consisting of information as to the data subject's political opinions that is carried out by certain people or political organisations where it does not cause nor is likely to cause substantial damage or substantial distress to the data subject or any other person.
- processing that:
  – is in the substantial public interest,
  – is necessary for research purposes (as defined in s 33 of the Act),
  – does not support measures or decisions with respect to any particular data subject otherwise than with the explicit consent of the data subject,
  – does not cause nor is likely to cause, substantial damage or substantial distress to the data subject or any other person.
- processing that is necessary for the exercise of any functions conferred on a constable by any rule of law.

7.8 Fifth Principle: Personal data shall not be kept for longer than is necessary

The Fifth Data Protection Principle provides that: 'Personal data processed for any purpose or purposes shall not be kept for longer than is necessary for that purpose or those purposes'.

To comply with this Principle, data controllers will need to review personal data regularly and to delete the information which is no longer required for their purposes, e.g. when an employee leaves. It may not be necessarily to delete all the personal data held in such circumstances. It may be necessary to keep some of the information regarding the individual's employment to provide references in the future or to enable the employer to provide the relevant information for pension arrangements. In some cases it may also be necessary to retain certain information for the purposes of defending legal claims which may be made in the future. Unless there is some other reason for keeping them, the personal data should be deleted when the possibility of a claim arising no longer exists, i.e. when the relevant statutory time limit has expired.

The value of records for historical purposes can also be taken into account. The Act provides that personal data processed only for historical, statistical or research purposes in compliance with the conditions set out in s 33, may be kept indefinitely. (Section 33(3)).

7.9 Seventh Principle: Data security

The Seventh Data Protection Principle requires appropriate technical and organisational measures to be taken to prevent unauthorised or unlawful processing of personal data and accidental loss or destruction of, or damage to, personal data.

The Act gives some further guidance on matters which should be taken into account in deciding whether security measures are 'appropriate'. These are as follows:

(i) Taking into account the state of technological development at any time and the cost of implementing any measures, the measures must ensure a level of security appropriate to:

   (a) the harm that might result from a breach of security; and

   (b) the nature of the data to be protected.

(ii) The data controller must take reasonable steps to ensure the reliability of staff having access to the personal data.

Standard risk assessment and risk management techniques need to be applied for these purposes to identify potential threats to the system, the vulnerability of the system to those threats and the counter-measures needed to reduce and manage the risk. In many cases, a simple consideration of these matters will be sufficient.

According to guidance issued by the Information Commissioner, questions which data controllers should consider for these purposes include:

- Security management
  - Does the data controller have a security policy setting out management commitment to information security within the organisation?
  - Is responsibility for the organisation's security policy clearly placed on a particular person or department?
  - Are sufficient resources and facilities made available to enable that responsibility to be fulfilled?
- Controlling access to information
  - Is access to the building or room controlled or can anybody walk in?
  - Can casual passers-by read information off screens or documents?
  - Are passwords known only to authorised people and are the passwords changed regularly?
  - Do passwords give access to all levels of the system or only to those personal data with which that employee should be concerned?
  - Is there a procedure for cleaning media (such as tapes and disks) before they are reused or are new data merely written over old? In the latter case is there a possibility of the old data reaching somebody who is not authorised to receive it? (e.g. as a result of the disposal of redundant equipment).
  - Is printed material disposed of securely, for example, by shredding?
  - Is there a procedure for authenticating the identity of a person to whom personal data may be disclosed over the telephone prior to the disclosure of the personal data?
  - Is there a procedure covering the temporary removal of personal data from the data controller's premises, for example, for staff to work on at home? What security measures are individual members of staff required to take in such circumstances?
  - Are responsibilities for security clearly defined between a data processor and its customers?

- Ensuring business continuity
  - Are the precautions against burglary, fire or natural disaster adequate?
  - Is the system capable of checking that the data are valid and initiating the production of back-up copies? If so, is full use made of these facilities?
  - Are back-up copies of all the data stored separately from the live files?
  - Is there protection against corruption by viruses or other forms of intrusion?
- Staff selection and training
  - Is proper weight given to the discretion and integrity of staff when they are being considered for employment or promotion or for a move to an area where they will have access to personal data?
  - Are the staff aware of their responsibilities? Have they been given adequate training and is their knowledge kept up-to-date?
  - Do disciplinary rules and procedures take account of the requirements of the Act? Are these rules enforced?
  - Does an employee found to be unreliable have his or her access to personal data withdrawn immediately?
  - Are staff made aware that data should only be accessed for business purposes and not for their own private purposes?
- Detecting and dealing with breaches of security
  - Do systems keep audit trails so that access to personal data is logged and can be attributed to a particular person?
  - Are breaches of security properly investigated and remedied; particularly when damage or distress could be caused to an individual?

The Act introduces express obligations upon data controllers when the processing of personal data is carried out by a data processor on behalf of the data controller. To comply with the Seventh Principle the data controller must:

- choose a data processor providing sufficient guarantees in respect of the technical and organisational security measures they take;
- take reasonable steps to ensure compliance with those measures; and
- ensure that the processing by the data processor is carried out under a contract, which is made or evidenced in writing, under which the

data processor is to act only on instructions from the data controller. The contract must require the data processor to comply with obligations equivalent to those imposed on the data controller by the Seventh Principle.

Further guidance on data security can be found in BS 7799 and 1S0/IEC Standard 17799 (see **Appendix B**).

7.10 Exemptions

Part IV of the Act (ss 28–36 and Sch 7) provides a number of exemptions from various provisions of the Act. For example, where a data controller is obliged by or under any enactment to make personal data available to the public, it is exempt from:

- the subject information provisions;
- the Fourth Principle (accuracy);
- section 12A of the Act (exempt manual data during transitional periods);
- sections 14(1)–(3) of the Act (rectification, blocking, erasure and destruction); and
- the non-disclosure provisions.

Where the disclosure is required by or under any enactment, by any rule of law or by the order of a court, personal data is exempt from the non-disclosure provisions.

In addition, there is no requirement to notify where the sole purpose of any processing is the maintenance of a public register.

7.11 Guidance on application to employment records

The Information Commissioner has issued *The Employment Practices Data Protection Code*, which provides guidance on the application of the Data Protection Act to employment records. The Code has four parts:

- Part 1: Recruitment and selection
- Part 2: Employment records
- Part 3: Monitoring at work
- Part 4: Information about workers' health.

7.12 Use of personal data for direct marketing

Prior consent is required for certain types of direct marketing under the Privacy and Electronic Communications (EC Directive) Regulations 2003 (see further *Guidance to the Privacy and Electronic Communications (EC Directive) Regulations 2003* issued by the Information Commissioner). Marketing departments may not send direct marketing communications to anyone who has informed them directly that they no longer wish to receive them or to anyone who has registered such a preference with a service such as the telephone preference service or the fax preference service.

8 Storage of records

8.1 Introduction

Information can be stored in a document in many different ways and in many different forms. The word 'document' is defined in several UK statutes as 'anything in which information of any description is recorded'. This recognises that information could be contained in a standard paper document, map, plan, photograph, tape, recording, film, microfilm, fax, computer file and a whole host of other non-conventional sources.

This chapter examines the various issues connected with the storage of records, including:

- choice of media (see **8.2**);
- the characteristics of paper records (see **8.3**);
- microfilm records (see **8.4**) and procedures to ensure that they are admissible as evidence (see **8.5**);
- storage conditions for records (see **8.6**).

Electronic records are covered separately in **Chapter 9**.

8.2 Choice of media

These days, most business records are created using computer software (e.g. correspondence created using a word processor) and many will remain in electronic form throughout their life (e.g. software accounting ledgers). In general, documents received from third parties will usually be in paper form (e.g. purchase invoices), whereas documents and records created internally are more likely to be created and held in electronic form.

Where a choice of media is possible, that choice for records storage and retention purposes will depend on a range of factors, including:

- the original media and the options available for the type of information it contains;
- the need to be able to freeze the information (i.e. to create a record);
- business needs such as:
    - frequency of use and referral,

- ease of access for users,
- the need to be able manipulate the information for management or reporting purposes.
- the relative costs of storage and transfer to different media;
- the reliability of the transfer process;
- the purpose for which the record is to be retained;
- the retention period;
- any special legal or regulatory requirements as to the form in which it ought to be retained.

i   Original media and type of information

Retaining a document or record in its original form helps to avoid conversion costs and eliminate any doubts as to the validity or reliability of copies. However, it will not always be the most appropriate method for storage nor the most cost effective.

The options available in each case will depend on the nature of the information which needs to be stored and how it was created or received. For example, photographs taken using traditional film could be stored as negatives or prints or converted into digital form. Photographs taken using a digital camera could be stored in their original digital form (e.g. on the digital film/memory card), copied to some other digital media or retained as prints.

For documents created internally using computer software, it may not always be obvious which is the original – the computer file or the printed copy. Some organisations deliberately operate a print to paper policy and treat the paper records as the originals. However, the modern trend is to treat the computer file as the original wherever possible.

ii   Freezing a record

Documents that need to be retained for legal or regulatory purposes will normally need to be capable of being frozen as a record. This is particularly important in the case of documents created and stored on a computer. Raw computer files on a rewritable hard disk will not always be ideal for records retention purposes unless they are write-protected or, as in the case of sophisticated accounting or company secretarial software packages, a comprehensive audit trail is kept by the system of changes made to the data. Sometimes the software used to create a document may actually modify the information each time the document is opened. For example, this might happen where, a macro was used to insert the date in a document generated by a word processor or to make a calculation in a spreadsheet. In such cases it may be necessary to store the file in some other way for records retention purposes.

iii Business needs

The need to manipulate information and to make it available within the business may influence the way in which it is kept. These issues may or may not determine how the original records should be kept for retention purposes. Sometimes, it will be necessary to operate a dual system whereby the original is kept for retention purposes but the information it contains is captured for distribution or manipulation.

A summary of the most important elements of paper documents received by an organisation is often captured by entering it into a database or software program so as to enable further analysis, manipulation, consolidation and comparisons to be made. For example, details of all purchase invoices are entered into software accounting ledgers. In this particular case, both the originals and the summary must be kept for specified periods. In some cases, however, it may suffice to keep the summary and in others, it may be necessary only to keep the originals.

iv Cost benefit

Records management policies are often directed towards minimising the costs of retaining paper records or finding a cost-effective alternative. The direct storage costs of paper records can be calculated fairly easily (see 8.3). Indirect costs, such as the salaries of registry and secretarial staff, are more difficult to quantify. However, these will need to be taken into account when assessing the merits of alternative systems because the indirect costs of those alternatives systems (such as the cost of capture) will probably be much more visible. Any decision to convert to a different system will almost certainly be influenced by other less tangible factors such as business efficiency and improvements in information flows.

v Reliability of transfer process

Strict procedures will need to be followed to ensure the security and integrity of records transferred from one media to another if the records will be required for any legal or regulatory reasons (see **9.5** and **9.6**). Reliability will be a particular problem where any form of optical character reading is involved.

vi Retention period

The media used to store records must be appropriate for the relevant retention period. Most paper records have a long life. However, thermally printed faxes and receipts deteriorate very quickly. Computer media usually has a limited useful life. Manufacturers often quote figures for mean time between failures or the average number of times the media may be accessed reliably. Any such failure would be catastrophic. Accordingly it will always be necessary to keep back-up copies of data and may be necessary to transfer that data to new media occasionally. These limitations have helped to prolong the life of microfiche as a long-term storage solution.

8.3 Paper

Paper is not a perfect storage medium. It can deteriorate over time depending on the quality of the paper and the method of printing (e.g. thermal fax paper can deteriorate in less than a year). This and many of the other relatively mundane issues associated with the storage of paper records may need to be addressed in records management policies and procedures. For example, the policy might specify:

- documents and records which should be kept in fire resistant safes and cabinets;
- file security for different classes of records;
- records which should be kept in a central registry;
- filing conventions;
- file indexing and identification;
- file access;
- procedures for deposit and retrieval of records to and from a central depository.

Staff are most likely to need to refer to records early on in their life, so during this initial period it is sensible to store them close at hand or make them readily available by some other means, e.g. via a computer network or microfiche records. Establishing a central registry for current records may help to reduce the volume of paper records that need to be stored where more than one department at the same site needs access to them. Consideration should, of course, be given to the effect such a policy might have on operational efficiency. The records may be needed on a regular basis by a particular department for only a short period, so the fact that they are available in a central registry may allow the duplicates to be destroyed earlier. A central registry may be required where security considerations dictate a higher degree of control over access. Central registry staff may also be able to undertake many of the administrative tasks associated with the implementation of the retention policies, relieving operational staff of this burden.

The number of referrals to records usually diminishes over time until it is no longer possible to justify storage at operational sites. In large organisations, where the cost of record retention is significant, the number and type of referrals may be analysed and kept under review to establish the most cost-effective and efficient storage solution. However, most organisations have to rely on the practical experience of users who tend to exaggerate the importance of records by concentrating on the exceptions rather than the rule. This is even more likely where they find it difficult or time-consuming to gain access to records once they have been removed.

For all but the smallest organisations, some form of centralised storage facility or depository will be required for records which are no longer necessary for routine operational purposes but, according to the policy, must be retained for other reasons. If a central depository is established, certain controls need to be established as part of the retention policy. These controls should cover:

- the documents which should be deposited;
- timings and frequency of deposit;
- access procedures, particularly for commercially sensitive or confidential records.

The choice of central depository may be limited by the nature of the record being retained, its commercial sensitivity and actual business location. Fire is an ever-present business risk and it may be desirable to have records stored off-site so that they are not lost in such an event. Many commercial organisations and these provide this type of service which can be used where it would be too expensive to establish one. The organisation's retention policy should be agreed before any comparative shopping between competing storage providers is undertaken. The policy can then be used as part of the specification for the purposes of obtaining of any quotes and in the final contractual arrangements. Availability to the user, frequency of possible use and the flow of records in and out of the central storage point are all matters of concern in making the choice. Such factors may be hard to define in financial terms.

It is relatively easy to assess the cost (or potential cost) of storage at operational sites by apportioning accommodation costs. However, removing records will not necessarily reduce those costs unless some alternative economic use can be found for the space saved. The final decision might be influenced by a desire to improve the working environment.

i Costs

An analysis of the costs of the records operations should be an integral part of an information survey (see **2.3**). Background information needs to be obtained from a central source and used in conjunction with the results of the survey as part of the overall evaluation and report.

Accommodation costs vary from building to building and location to location. For example, office accommodation is usually considerably more expensive than storage accommodation simply because of the nature of the services required by each (telecommunications, electricity, lighting, etc).

Equipment costs are crucial to an evaluation of a survey's results. Some types of equipment are more cost-effective than others (for example lateral filing cupboards compared to four-drawer filing cabinets) and a careful analysis of their relative costs, including any maintenance, is important for reaching cost-effective solutions or improvements in records management procedures.

Comparison of storage costs is most easily achieved by calculating a storage factor for each type of equipment. This is simply the result of dividing the amount of files (in linear metres) by the area occupied (in square metres), including the area necessary to access the records. The higher the storage factor the more efficient is the equipment. For example:

- a four-drawer filing cabinet holds 2.5 m of records and occupies 2.25 sq m of space; the storage factor is therefore 1.11;

- a lateral filing cupboard holds 4 m of records and occupies 0.77 sq m of space; the storage factor is therefore 5.2.

8.4 Microfilm

There are many different kinds of microfilm or microfiche, some of which are produced directly from data held on computer so that the microfilm becomes the only visible or tangible record. The advantages of microfilmed records over paper records in terms of storage are obvious.

A careful analysis of the cost benefits of microfilming should be undertaken. Labour and equipment costs must be taken into account together with the effect microfilming is likely to have on operational or administrative efficiency. Microfilming is most suitable for storing large volumes of similar records which can be indexed fairly easily. It is less suitable for records where the important evidential value is a signature, records vary in size or where the originals are of poor quality.

If the records are to be retained for legal reasons, strict procedures must be followed (see **8.5** below).

8.5 Microfilm as evidence

Copies of documentary evidence held on microfilm are admissible as evidence under the Civil Evidence Act 1995 whether or not they are hearsay, provided that they are authenticated. In criminal proceedings, microfilm copies of business documents will generally be admissible under s 27 of the Criminal Justice Act 1988 if properly authenticated, although, if the evidence they contain is hearsay, they will be subject to the conditions of ss 23 and 24 of that Act (see **5.9**). Section 71 of the Police and Criminal Evidence Act 1984 also makes specific provision to allow the contents of a document, whether or not it is still in existence, to be proved by the production of an enlargement of a microfilm copy authenticated in such manner as the court may approve.

The British Standards Institute has issued guidance on microform procedures (*BS 6498:2002 – Guide to preparation of microfilm and other microforms that may be required as evidence*). Although, compliance with the standard cannot guarantee that a document held in microform will be admissible as evidence, it should ensure that a microfilm copy of a document is not rendered inadmissible for lack of authentication.

The standard recommends the establishment of a comprehensive microform programme which includes all feasible safeguards to establish that a microform made in accordance with the programme is a true copy of the original records.

The document that records the policy decision made by or on behalf of an organisation to establish a microform programme should be retained permanently. Written authority within the terms of this authorising document should be issued, nominating the members of staff responsible for implementing and operating the programme, signing documents relating to it, and ensuring that standards are maintained, whether the microforms are prepared within the organisation or by a bureau.

A document setting out the organisation's plan for a microform programme should be prepared and should include:

- the categories of original to be microfilmed;
- the stage at which the original should be microfilmed;
- the procedures for microfilming, including certification, checking and information retrieval methods;
- provision for a register to be maintained;
- the periods of retention of originals and microforms;
- provision for the destruction of originals and for recording their destruction;
- provision for review of the programme.

When the plan has been approved, the organisation should authorise, in writing, the introduction of a microform programme as part of its customary activity from a specified date.

A manual should be prepared giving detailed instructions to staff concerned in the various stages of the microform programme including information about:

- the equipment and microforms to be used;
- quality control;
- indexing;
- correction of errors, including rules for splicing;
- routine monitoring;
- production of full-size prints from microforms, if required.

Various forms may be needed when operating a microform programme, including:

- a certificate of authority for microfilming;
- a camera operator's certificate;
- a certificate of destruction;
- a certificate of acceptance.

(See examples at **Appendix C**.)

The programme should include requirements for establishing a register in which the following should be recorded:

- the identification reference of the original document;
- the date and reference of the certificate of authority;
- the date and reference of the camera operator's certificate;
- the date and reference of the certificate of destruction;
- the reference(s) of the microform(s);
- the date and reference of the certificate of acceptance (if one is required);
- the storage location of the original microform(s) and duplicates.

Several other British and International Standards deal with microform equipment and media, preparation of copy for imaging and the presentation of data on microforms (See **Appendix B.**)

Computer output to microfilm (COM) may be treated in the same way as a computer printout, i.e. as an original rather than a copy. If computer-generated information on paper would be acceptable, the same information on COM should be equally acceptable, provided that the image is satisfactory. However, if the information transferred to microform during this process was itself a copy, the COM output would also need to be treated as a copy.

8.6 Storage conditions

Records should be stored in appropriate conditions. These conditions for records should generally conform to industry standards. The BSI issues a number of standards regarding these matters for different types of media (see **Appendix B**).

9 Electronic records

9.1 Introduction

This chapter, deals with particular issues arising in relation to electronic records, including:

- the growth in their use for retention and business purposes (see **9.2**);
- software for specific retention purposes (see **9.3**);
- electronic document management and records management systems (see **9.4**);
- types of electronic media (see **9.5**);
- the BSI Code on the legal admissibility of records stored electronically (see **9.6**);
- electronic signatures (see **9.8**).

9.2 Electronic records

Any business which has a computer is likely to need to treat at least some of the information held on that computer as a record for retention purposes. The only way to avoid this is to adopt a universal print-to-paper policy. Such a policy is unlikely to be practical where, for example, specialist accounting software is used to maintain the accounting ledgers.

Various technological developments in computer hardware and software have increased the availability and capacity for records retention and decreased the need for retaining hard copies.

It has been possible to keep accounting records on a computer for many years and tax legislation now specifically provides for the retention of electronic copies of supporting documents and vouchers. Original vouchers are however still required in a few selected areas (see **Chapter 14**).

Similar provision is now made to allow records to be kept on computer for a variety of other legislative purposes, to the extent that it is now becoming difficult to find examples of requirements to retain paper originals (see generally Part II). This trend is likely to continue and policies need to be kept under constant review to maximise the benefit of these developments and to reduce the retention of paper documents.

Various software systems can now be used to eliminate paper from the workplace and to satisfy retention requirements. Software for these purposes can be divided up into two main categories:

- systems specifically designed to keep records such as statutory registers, accounts and payroll records;
- electronic document management systems.

9.3 Software for specific records retention purposes

Computer software that is specifically designed to keep certain registers and records in compliance with regulatory requirements may need to comply with certain guidelines set by regulatory authorities, who may even specify compliant systems or certify them. This is certainly true of company secretarial software and, to a lesser extent, of accounting and payroll packages. System providers usually state whether their systems are compliant in marketing literature. If they do not, the system may not be compliant. It will often be necessary to upgrade the software elements of any system in order to remain compliant. Such systems and the procedures for operating them will also probably need to comply with the BSI's *Code of Practice for Legal Admissibility of Information Stored Electronically* (see **9.6**).

9.4 Electronic document and records management systems

Electronic Document Management (EDM) and Electronic Record Management (ERM) are closely related functions. which can often, but are not always, found in one integrated software package. They support the management of electronic information in different, but complementary, ways.

i Electronic document management

Electronic document management helps organisations to exploit their information more effectively by providing better access to stored information and by supporting teams working together with workflow software. It generally supports the immediate operational requirement for business information but may not support all of the records management functions.

Typically, electronic document management systems will capture paper or electronic documents and provide for:

- storage and indexing at the document level;
- search and retrieval at the document level;
- access management and security control;
- off-line archiving for semi-active or inactive documents;
- version control;
- audit trails on access and changes to the document;
- document profiles (information about the document);
- integration with document image processing and workflow systems.

ii Electronic records management

Electronic records management (ERM) provides an environment for capturing electronic documents and applying standard records management practices. It generally supports the medium to long-term information management needs of the business. It manages a corporate filing structure, document classification within the filing structure, and formal retention and disposition scheduling based on an approved disposition and review schedule.

Typical requirements for electronic records management, in addition to those already given for electronic document management, are to support:

- capturing, storing, indexing and retrieving all elements of the record as a complex unit, and for all types of record;
- management of records within class categories or filing structures to maintain the narrative links between records;
- record level metadata describing contextual information;
- integration between electronic and paper records;
- secure storage and management to ensure authenticity and accountability, including support for legal and regulatory requirements;
- appraisal and selection of records;
- systematic retention and disposition of records;
- migration and export of records for permanent preservation.

An ERM system must preserve the content, structure and context of the electronic records, ensure that records are 'registered' and that authentication procedures and audit trails are put in place. In turn, this will permit these records to be used as legal evidence, improve corporate accountability and assist organisations in meeting the requirements of internal and external auditors.

Increasingly, electronic document management packages are extending their facilities into the area of ERM, often by incorporating independent specialist packages, and thereby offering an integrated system.

iii Designing electronic records management into systems

It is important to ensure that in all new systems work, the ability to manage electronic records is properly taken into account. Often, electronic records management requirements are not sufficiently recognised in determining the functional requirements for a new or upgraded system, and have not been given a high enough priority in the design and development of information systems. The functional requirements necessary for managing and preserving records can be built into the design and implementation of electronic systems more easily, and less expensively, if they are identified at an early stage.

Records of any type kept on a computer ought to be kept in a manner that is acceptable to regulatory authorities and ensures that they will be admissible as evidence in legal proceedings. In the latter case compliance with the BSI's *Code of Practice for Legal Admissibility of Information Stored Electronically* will almost certainly be necessary (see **9.6**).

9.5 Electronic media

Electronic records may be held in a variety of forms including optical disk (including CDs and DVD), mainframe memory, computer tapes and standard PC floppy disks.

One of the main problems with electronic storage is ensuring and proving the integrity of the data. Generally speaking, this will be easier where the media is not re-writable. This type of media is sometimes referred to as WORM media (Write-Once-Read-Many). The use of such media is plainly not possible for living records such as databases.

Electronic media is rarely as stable as paper or microfilm. Any fault or damage to it can cause a catastrophic loss of data. Accordingly, it will always be necessary to keep back-up copies of electronic records. Where electronic media is used for long-term storage purposes, it may also be necessary to transfer the records to new media if the original media is reaching the end of its reliable life.

A further complication that needs to be addressed when using electronic media for records storage purposes is the possibility that developments in hardware and software technologies may make it impossible to access the records in their original form. Attempts can be made to migrate the records into new systems. However, on occasion, the only practical answer might be to retain the original hardware and software. This is plainly not a very satisfactory solution as the relevant systems may be old, bulky and may become unreliable over time. These issues tend to dictate that records should be stored in industry-standard and commonly used formats that are software independent, although this will not always be possible.

Another danger with any electronic system is, of course, that the supplier of the hardware or software system or the media used to store records may simply go out of business or stop manufacturing that product. Although this can normally be remedied, it may be costly to do so. These issues would seem to suggest that there can be dangers in being an early adopter of new technology, particularly if it is purchased from a small supplier. The old principle that 'no-one ever got sacked for buying . . .' should perhaps be borne in mind here.

9.6 BSI Code on legal admissibility of information stored electronically

Compliance with the British Standards Institute's *Code of Practice for Legal Admissibility of Information Stored Electronically* will help to ensure that electronic records are not only admissible as evidence in UK courts but also given due weight. The Code was first published in 1996 under the BSI reference BSI-DISC PD 0008. This reference was also used for the second edition published in 1999. However, for the third edition of the Code, published in 2004, the BSI adopted a new reference: BIP 0008.

The first edition of the Code, published in February 1996 under the title *Code of Practice for Legal Admissibility of Information Stored on Electronic Document Management Systems*, covered information stored on Write-Once-Read-Many (WORM) optical storage systems. The second edition, published in 1999, was extended to cover any type of electronic storage medium, including those that are rewritable. The latest edition is more of an editorial revision than a technical one. However, it does make the following technical changes:

- reference is made to issues raised by BS ISO 15489 *Records management*;
- a section has been added on data file capture;
- the section on digital and electronic signatures has been updated;
- audit requirements for specific document 'types' have been added;
- the chapter on 'audit trails' has been restructured and includes some new recommendations.

The Code describes the means by which it may be demonstrated at any time, in a manner acceptable to a court of law that:

- the contents of a specific data file created or existing within a computer system have not changed since the time of storage; and
- where such a data file contains a digitised image of a physical source document, the digitised image is a true facsimile of that source document.

A 'data file' is defined in the Code as a collection of 'related data handled as a discrete unit' (e.g. a word processor file or a file containing an image of a document).

The Code is structured in accordance with the five principles defined in BSI-DISC PD 0010 '*Principles of Good Practice for Information Management*'. These principles, which act as guidelines for the procedures and controls required, are as follows:

- recognise and understand all types of information;
- understand the legal issues and execute duty of care responsibilities;
- identify and specify business processes and procedures;
- identify enabling technologies to support business processes and procedures;
- monitor and audit business processes and procedures.

i   Principle 1: Recognise and understand

In relation to the first principle, the Code recommends that senior management should adopt, and regularly review, an Information Management Policy Document. This Policy Document should:

- Specify what information is covered:

- information should be grouped into 'types', the policy for all information within a 'type' being consistent;
- the policy should list all 'types' of information which are to be stored in compliance with the BSI Code;
- it should include as an information 'type' all documents produced in compliance with the BSI Code (e.g. the Information Management Policy Document).

- State, where appropriate, policy regarding the security classification of each information 'type'.
- State policy regarding storage media including:
  - the media to be used for different information storage requirements;
  - the media on which each information type may be stored;
  - the policy for tracking data files.
- State policy regarding data file formats for each information 'type', data compression techniques and version control.
- State policy regarding relevant information management standards (e.g. BS EN ISO 9000).
- Define retention periods and destruction policies for each information 'type'.
- Define responsibilities for information management functions.
- Define responsibilities for compliance with the Code.

ii Principle 2: Legal issues and duty of care

The Code recommends that organisations should adopt an Information Security Policy which should, as a minimum, set out:
- the scope of the policy;
- a statement of management objectives in respect of security;
- specific policy statements;
- requirements for different information categories;
- definition and allocation of information security responsibilities;
- policies for dealing with breaches of security;
- policy regarding compliance with relevant standards.

The Code also recommends:
- the adoption of a Disaster Recovery Plan, which should be tested to ensure that the integrity of stored information is not compromised if put into effect; and

- that organisations should take into account the external implications of using electronic information management systems by consulting with any relevant regulatory or government bodies, auditors and legal advisors, etc.

iii Principle 3: Processes and procedures

The Code recommends that organisations should maintain a Procedures Manual for each information management system complying with the Code, describing all procedures related to the operation and use of the system, including:

- information capture;
- indexing;
- authenticated output procedures;
- authentication of copies of data files;
- file transmission;
- information retention;
- disposal;
- backup and system recovery;
- system maintenance;
- security and protection;
- outsourcing;
- workflow;
- self-modifying files;
- date and time stamps;
- voice, audio and video data;
- version control;
- maintenance of documentation.

iv Principle 4: Enabling technologies

The Code recommends that a description of hardware, software and network elements that comprise the system and how they interact should be included in a Systems Description Manual. The Manual should:

- contain details of system configurations;
- contain details of all changes to the system and of any processes implemented to effect the change;
- be structured so that details of the system at any time during the period of its use may be determined.

v Principle 5: Monitor and audit

When preparing information for use as evidence, it is often necessary to provide supporting data such as the date of storage, details of movement from medium to medium, and evidence of the controlled operation of the system. These details are known as audit trail information. The Code requires sufficient audit trail information to be kept to enable the authenticity of stored information to be proved. Audit trail data on both the system and the stored information will be necessary for these purposes.

9.7 BS 7799 'A Code of Practice for Information Security Management'

Information and knowledge play an increasingly important role in the modern business environment and need to be protected in the same way as a business would protect any other assets. Modern technology enables information to be stored, transmitted, and retrieved more easily, potentially increasing its value to the organisation. However, it also introduces new threats to the security of that information. These threats can be internal, external, accidental, or malicious. To protect against them, organisations need to establish and implement a comprehensive Information Security Policy. There is no need to reinvent the wheel in this regard. The BSI publishes standards and guidance to assist in this process. Its Information Security Standard is published in two parts:

- ISO/IEC 17799 Code of Practice for Information Security Management.
- BS 7799-2:2002 Specification for Information Security Management.

The standard sets out the requirements for an Information Security Management System and helps to identify, manage and minimise the range of threats to which information is regularly subjected. Annex A of BS 7799 identifies 10 controls:

- security policy;
- organisation of assets and resources;
- asset classification and control;
- personnel security;
- physical and environmental security;
- communications and operations management – to ensure the

correct and secure operation of information processing facilities;
- access control;
- systems development and maintenance – to ensure that security is built into information systems;
- business continuity management – to counteract interruptions to business activities and to protect critical business processes from the effects of major failures or disasters;
- compliance – to avoid breaches of any criminal and civil law, statutory, regulatory or contractual obligations, and any security requirement.

An organisation using BS 7799 as the basis for its Information Security Management System can become registered by the BSI. Registration obviously demonstrates the organisation's commitment to information security, and may be demanded by customers and suppliers, particularly when systems for electronic commerce are being established. Registration and compliance with the standard should also help to ensure that electronic records will be admissible as evidence in legal proceedings and given full weight.

9.8 Electronic signatures

Section 7 of the Electronic Communications Act 2000 makes provision for the admissibility in legal proceedings of electronic signatures and the certification by any person of such a signature. Both are admissible in evidence in relation to any of the following questions as to the authenticity or integrity of the communication or data to which they relate:
- whether it comes from a particular person or other source;
- whether it is accurately timed and dated;
- whether it is intended to have legal effect; and
- whether there has been any tampering with or other modification of the communication or data.

An electronic signature is defined in s 7(2) of the Electronic Communications Act 2000 as so much of anything in electronic form as it:
- is incorporated into or otherwise logically associated with any electronic communication or electronic data; and
- purports to be so incorporated or associated for the purpose of being used in establishing the authenticity of the communication or data, the integrity of the communication or data, or both.

This definition allows a variety of different methods to be used to apply an electronic signature. However, the security of the method used may have a bearing on the weight given in legal proceedings to any evidence authenticated by an electronic signature. To ensure that an electronic signature is given at least the same (if not more) weight than a manual signature, the most up-to-date cryptographic techniques must be used. These ensure that the document may only be unlocked by applying the public key of the person who encrypted it. If the document can be opened using the public key of the person who sent it, it must also have been encrypted using that person's private key. Using this type of electronic signature also ensures that the message cannot be tampered with before being opened by the recipient. Most, but not all, electronic signatures are provided by commercial organisations who are able to provide a measure of assurance to third parties that an electronic signature belongs to the person that it purports to represent. They cannot, however, provide any assurance as to whether the signature was applied by, or on behalf of, its owner.

The Electronic Communications Act 2000 provides that a person may certify an electronic signature by making a statement (whether before or after the making of the communication) confirming that the signature, a means of producing, communicating or verifying the signature, or a procedure applied to the signature, is (either alone or in combination with other factors) a valid means of establishing the authenticity of the communication or data, the integrity of the communication or data, or both (s 7(3)). A person could certify an electronic signature applied using an insecure method under this procedure. Difficulties may arise, however, where there is some dispute as to the validity of the electronic signature or as to whether the electronic signature was applied by or on behalf of the person it purports to represent.

Where a company may need to rely on the validity of an electronic signature in legal proceedings, it should generally insist that a secure method be used by the person applying it. This is certainly desirable where minutes are to be signed by the chairman using an electronic signature. It may, however, be impractical for some purposes. For example, most companies are likely to accept electronic proxy appointments authenticated by a personal identification number. Although this type of authentication would still be capable of being tendered as evidence in legal proceedings, a person seeking to challenge the validity of the appointment would probably find it much easier to undermine its evidential value. This is probably a risk that companies can afford to take as there is normally little likelihood that a forged proxy could affect the outcome of a meeting.

The Companies Act 1985 makes no provision to allow a company to act by electronic signature. However, any person authorised to sign documents or execute contracts on behalf of the company may do so by electronic signature, provided that the other party is willing to accept execution in this manner. In the case of documents that must be filed at Companies House, the Registrar has power to issue directions regarding authentication procedures.

It is possible for a person to authorise someone else to apply their electronic signature. Where this is done, it will be necessary to retain evidence of the authority given.

10 Life of a company

In many cases, the retention requirement for certain records is expressed in this book as being the 'life of the company'. In fact, it may be necessary to keep certain documents beyond the life of a company, i.e. after it has been wound up or struck off. Special provision is made in insolvency legislation to allow the liquidator of a company to dispose of its books and records after it has been wound up. No such provision is made for companies that have been struck off. However, in both cases, it is possible to identify certain records that must be retained.

10.1 Winding up

For companies in the process of liquidation (other than a members' voluntary liquidation), liquidators are required to keep certain records for six years after they cease to hold office, or to hand them over to their successor or to the Official Receiver (Insolvency Regulations 1994, regs 10–13).

In a winding up by the court, the liquidator on the authorisation of the official receiver, or the Official Receiver himself while acting as liquidator, may at any time sell destroy or otherwise dispose of the books, papers and other records of the company (Insolvency Regulations 1996, reg 16(1)).

The person who was the last liquidator of a company which has been dissolved under a members' voluntary liquidation or a creditors' voluntary liquidation may destroy or otherwise dispose of the books, papers and other records of the company one year after the date of dissolution (Insolvency Regulations 1994, reg 16(2)).

The court may, however, declare the dissolution of a company void on the application of the liquidator or any other interested person made up to two years after the date of dissolution. This time limit does not apply to an application for the purpose of bringing proceedings for damages for personal injury under s 1(2) of the Law Reform (Miscellaneous Provisions) Act 1934 or for damages under the Fatal Accidents Act 1976 or the Damages (Scotland) Act 1976, provided that an action would not be time-barred under the relevant legislation (CA 1985, s 651).

10.2 Striking off

No special provision is made in any legislation for the disposal of the books and records of a company that has been struck off. Accordingly, records for which the law provides for a specific retention period should almost certainly be kept for the prescribed period. This would apply, for example, to accounting and tax records and certain health and safety records. Some records might need to be handed over to a regulatory authority, e.g. site records under waste disposal regulations. Failure by a company that has been struck off to comply with the relevant retention requirements could result in the prosecution of its directors and officers. The Companies Act specifically provides that the liability of any director, managing officer or member of a company that has been struck off continues and may be enforced as if the company had not been dissolved (CA, ss 652(6)) and 652A(6)).

A company may be restored to the register up to 20 years after it was struck off on an application by the company, any member or creditor and various other people, or if the court considers it just to do so (CA, s 653). On restoration, any proceedings may be taken against the company or by the company that might have been taken if it had not been dissolved. One of the most common reasons for restoration is to enable a claim to be made on an insurance policy. It is questionable whether an application to strike off a company should be made at all if it is reasonably foreseeable that a claim might be made on an insurance policy. In any case, it would be prudent to retain copies of any insurance policies under which claims can still be made.

The statutory registers and records of a company that has been struck off (excluding those for which a specific retention period is provided, e.g. accounting records) would appear to serve very little purpose. The primary purpose of statutory registers is to make the required infor-mation entered in them available for inspection at a location in the country of incorporation. When a company has been struck off, the obligation to make them available for inspection no longer applies. Indeed, the only reasons for retaining them would appear to be that the Act does not specifically provide for their disposal, and the rather remote possibility that they might be needed if the company is restored to the register.

The most important registers could, if necessary, be recreated from records held at Companies House, e.g. the Register of Directors and Secretaries, the Register of Members (up to the date of the last Annual Return), and the Register of Charges (subject to the possible existence of charges not registered at Companies House). If any of these registers contain information not capable of being retrieved from Companies House, their retention should perhaps be considered. If they do not, there would seem to be no reason to retain them and we make no recommendation in this regard.

It would not be possible to recreate the Register of Directors' Interests in Shares or Debentures or, in the case of a public company, the Register of Substantial Interests in Voting Shares, except to the extent in both cases that the relevant interests were directly held. It is, however, highly unlikely that these registers would be needed even if the company was restored to the register for some reason. Accordingly, we make no specific recommendation for their retention beyond the life of the company.

Part II

Guidance on Retention Periods

11 Companies Act records

11.1 Statutory registers

The Companies Act 1985 requires companies to keep the following
statutory registers:

- Register of members;
- Register of mortgages and charges;
- Register of directors and secretaries;
- Register of directors' interests in shares or debentures;
- Register of substantial share interests (public companies only).

These must all be kept and made available for inspection by members and
others throughout the life of the company.

11.2 Other registers

Companies may keep various other registers that do not fall within the
definition of a statutory register in that the Act does not require them to
be kept. These may include:

i Register of Debenture Holders

The Act does not require a company to keep a register of debenture
holders, even if it has debentures in issue. Instead the question as to
whether a register must be kept will be determined by the terms of the
debenture issue. However, where a register is kept, the Act requires that
the register be made available for inspection. Thus, although this type of
register is treated as a statutory register for certain purposes, it is not
subject to the same retention requirements because the Act does not
require it to be kept (see **Chapter 12**).

ii Register of Directors' Interests in Transactions and the Register of Documents Sealed

These are commonly used to record information that can and should be
contained in the minutes of meetings of directors. The information is

entered in a register rather than the minutes (or in addition to the minutes) for convenience. They will, accordingly, need to be treated as a subset of the minutes (see **13.3**).

iii Register of Allotments and a Register of Transfers

These may be kept as part of the double entry system used for share registration. Although they are frequently included in combined registers published by legal stationers, they are not strictly statutory registers. They may need to be kept as a subset of the minutes if reference is made to them in the minutes for the purposes of approving allotments and share transfers. In addition, they will need to be kept for general share registration purposes (see **Chapter 12**).

Form of registers

Companies may keep their statutory registers either:
- by making entries in bound books; or
- in any other manner provided that adequate precautions are taken for guarding against falsification and for facilitating their discovery (CA, s 722).

The Act expressly states that this second option allows registers to be kept on a computer but imposes an additional condition in this case that they must be capable of being reproduced in legible form (s 723).

The above rules also apply to the Register of Debenture Holders and other statutory books and records such as registers which must be treated as a subset of the minutes.

Retention of registers

Statutory registers, and the information which they contain, must be kept for the life of the company. There are only two exceptions to this rule:
- *Register of debenture holders* – As there is no statutory requirement to keep a register of debenture holders, it is arguable that where one is kept it will not be necessary to retain it for any longer than would be necessary for limitation purposes.
- *Register of members* – Entries for former members may be deleted 20 years after a person ceases to be a member.

For all other statutory registers, entries should never be deleted even if they are no longer current. Instead, additional entries (such as the date of a director's resignation) should be made to enable the current position to be ascertained. It should also be possible with a little effort to determine from a register the information that was entered in it on any particular date during the company's life.

11.3 Statutory Returns

There is no statutory requirement to retain copies of company forms filed at Companies House, although it is probably sensible to do so for a short period. When filing statutory returns, most company secretaries include a covering letter on the company's headed notepaper naming the documents filed and requesting that Companies House confirm receipt of the relevant documents by endorsing and returning that covering letter. This receipt provides evidence, should it be needed, that the documents were delivered to Companies House on the date shown on the endorsed covering letter.

Where this system is operated, it is important to check that the necessary receipt is actually received and to investigate circumstances where it is not. If it transpires that Companies House did not actually receive the document, a further copy will need to be filed. More often than not, this will involve completing and obtaining the necessary signatures on a new form. The photocopy of the original may be helpful to prove that the company did its best to comply with the filing requirement, but will not be unacceptable as a substitute because original signatures are required on company forms. This would seem to suggest that if copies of company forms are to have maximum value, they should also be signed copies, although a copy of any form which was required to be stamped (e.g. Form 169) would presumably be acceptable as evidence that the necessary duty had been paid.

When a receipt is obtained from Companies House, the company can be certain that the return has been delivered on the date shown and that, if this is within the period for filing, it has complied with its obligations under the Companies Act 1985. It is not, however, necessarily safe to assume that the relevant return will ever be entered on the company's file. Although this is now rare, it is still possible for documents to go missing at Companies House or for them to be entered on the wrong company file or for there to be such a delay in entering them on the company's file that it appears that the document was not filed on time. Retention of the receipt issued by Companies House will ensure that the company is able to prove compliance with the relevant requirements.

If, as will usually be the case, the document is entered on the company's file at Companies House within the period for filing, there is no longer any real reason for retaining the receipt. This will involve checking Companies House records on a periodic basis or subscribing to one of the services offered by Companies House, such as Companies House Monitor or Companies House Direct.

Some statutory forms replicate the information that must be entered in a statutory register. For example, Forms 288a, b and c replicate the information required to be entered in the Register of Directors and Secretaries. Although not ideal, it is possible to file copies of these forms in a loose-leaf folder and to treat that folder and the forms as the Register of Directors and Secretaries. The same is true with forms filed in connection with company charges, although in this case additional information may need to be entered in the company's own register for charges that are not registered at Companies House. If copies of forms are retained for these purposes, they should obviously be retained for the life of the company. Even where a company makes other arrangements for keeping statutory registers, e.g. using computer software, copies of forms kept in such a manner could provide a back-up which might in itself provide sufficient justification for their retention.

Retention Schedule 1: Companies Act Records

Record Description	Regulatory retention period and source	Recommended retention period
Statutory Registers (see 11.1)		
1 Register of directors and secretaries	Life of company: [CA, s 288].	Same.
2 Register of directors' interests in shares and debentures	Life of company: [CA, s 325].	Same.
3 Notifications of interests in shares or debentures received from directors pursuant to ss 324-9		At least until change of interests entered in the register and disclosed in annual accounts.
4 Register of substantial interests in voting shares	Life of company: [CA, s 211].	Life of company.
5 Notifications of substantial interests or changes received pursuant to ss 198-210		At least until notification included in register and annual accounts.
6 Responses to s 212 notices	Life of company: [CA, s 213].	Same.
7 Register of charges	Life of company: [CA, s 411/ Scotland, s 422].	Same.
8 Copies of charge instruments or copy of one debenture of a series required to be made available for inspection	Life of company: [CA, s 406/ Scotland, s 421].	Same.
9 Register of members	See Retention Schedule 2 for details.	
10 Register of debentures or loan stock holders	None.	See Retention Schedule 2 for details.
11 Register of directors' declarations of interest		
12 Register of documents sealed		

Form in which to be kept	Reasons and remarks
In any form (including electronic) [CA, ss 722 and 723].	Info also filed at Companies House on Forms 288a, b and c. Entries for former directors and secretaries should not be deleted.
In any form (including electronic) [CA, ss 722 and 723].	Entries for former directors should not be deleted.
	Best practice. Can be useful for reconciling year-end balance. Directors may prefer company to keep longer to prove compliance.
In any form (including electronic) [CA, ss 722 and 723].	
No requirement to keep original.	Best practice.
In any form (including electronic) [CA, ss 722 and 723].	Responses must be entered in Register of substantial interests.
In any form (including electronic) [CA, ss 722 and 723].	Details of most charges also registered at Companies House. Entries in register cannot be deleted.
Copies, not originals, are required to be made available for inspection.	Originals will need to be kept for other purposes if the company has them.
In any form (including electronic) [CA, ss 722 and 723].	See Retention Schedule 2 for full details.
In any form (including electronic) [CA, ss 722 and 723].	See Retention Schedule 2 for details.
In any form (including electronic) [CA, ss 722 and 723].	See entry in Retention Schedule 3.
In any form (including electronic) [CA, ss 722 and 723].	See entry in Retention Schedule 3.

Retention Schedule 1: Companies Act Records – *continued*

Record Description	Regulatory retention period and source	Recommended retention period
Other Companies Act Records		
13 Certificate of incorporation		Life of company.
14 Certificate to commence business (plc only)		Life of company.
15 Certificate of change of company name		Life of company.
16 Memorandum of association		
– current version		A copy must be kept for practical business reasons and to enable compliance with CA, ss 19 and 20.
– signed copies of the original version		Usually for life of company.
– former versions		Usually for life of company.
17 Articles of association		
– current version		A copy must be kept for practical business reasons and to enable compliance with CA, ss 19 and 20.
– signed copies of the original version		Usually for life of company.
– former versions		Usually for life of company.
– copy signed for the purposes of identification		Usually for life of company.

Form in which to be kept	Reasons and remarks
Original required.	Evidence/ Implied by CA, s 13.
Original required.	Evidence/ Implied by CA, s 117.
Original required.	Evidence/Implied by CA, s 28.
Copies may be kept in any form.	To enable compliance – a copy of the current version should also have been filed at Companies House.
Usually kept in original form but need not be.	Evidence – although the original signed copy will have been filed at Companies House on incorporation, other signed copies may also have been produced and still be in the company's possession.
May be kept in any form.	Evidence – a copy of any amended version will have been filed at Companies House.
Copies may be kept in any form.	To enable compliance – a copy of the current version should also have been filed at Companies House.
Usually kept in original form but need not be.	Evidence – although the original signed copy may have been filed at Companies House on incorporation, other signed copies may also have been produced and still be in the company's possession.
May be kept in any form.	Evidence – a copy of any amended version will have been filed at Companies House.
Original.	Evidence.

Retention Schedule 1: Companies Act Records – *continued*

Record Description	Regulatory retention period and source	Recommended retention period
at the general meeting at which they were adopted		
18 Printed copies of resolutions filed at Companies House	Life of company: [CA, ss 20 and 380].	Life of company.
19 Shareholder agreements		
20 Directors' service contracts		Six years after cessation.
21 Contract for purchase of own shares (or memorandum of terms)	10 years from date of purchase: [CA, s 169].	Same.
Statutory Returns (see 11.3)		
22 Acknowledgements of receipt issued by Companies House in respect of filed documents		Until entry on Companies House file has been confirmed.
23 Form 169 (purchase of own shares)		Copies should be kept for at least six years.
24 Annual return		Three years.
25 Form 88(2): Returns of allotments		Until entry on Companies House file has been confirmed.
26 Forms 288a, b and c (Directors and Secretaries)		Until entry on Companies House file has been confirmed.
27 Copies of other statutory returns filed at Companies House		Should be kept until entry on Companies House file has been confirmed.

Form in which to be kept	Reasons and remarks
May be kept in any form.	Resolutions must also be incorporated in Mem and Arts.
	Limitation/Tax Current contracts of over 12 months' duration must be made available for inspection under CA, s 318.
CA only requires a copy to be kept.	Statutory.
Original recommended.	
Original must be filed at Companies House, so copy in any form will suffice.	Provides evidence of payment of stamp duty.
Original must be filed at Companies House, so copy in any form will suffice.	Previous three years' returns may be useful when compiling future returns.
Original must be filed at Companies House, so copy in any form will suffice.	May be longer if the return is the only prime record of the allotment.
Original must be filed at Companies House, so copy in any form will suffice.	Details from these forms should be entered in the Register of directors and secretaries. Copies of the forms entered in a loose-leaf folder could constitute the register required to be kept under s 288.
Original must be filed at Companies House, so copy in any form will suffice.	

12 Share registration and dividends

12.1 The register of members

A member is defined in s 22(2) of the Companies Act 1985 (CA) as a person who has agreed to become a member and whose name has been entered in the company's register of members. Section 361 provides that the register of members is *prima facie* evidence of any matters which are directed or authorised by the Act to be entered in it. This means that in legal proceedings the entries in a company's register of members will be assumed to be correct unless evidence to the contrary can be shown.

Section 352 establishes the basic requirement to keep and make up the register of members. The register must contain details of both current and former members, although entries relating to former members can be removed 20 years after they ceased to be a member (CA, s 352(6)). The register may be kept in a bound book, ring binder or on computer, but must be capable of being reproduced in legible form (CA, ss 722 and 723). In view of its special evidential status, it is particularly important that the register is kept securely to prevent falsification.

Despite the fact that the register of members is given special evidential status in law, it is advisable for a company to keep certain documents as supporting evidence of the entries made in its register. To assess what should be kept and for how long, it is necessary to understand the nature of a company's liabilities, the actions it could face and the limitation periods for each type of action. This is a very complex area, and it is only possible here to give a summary of the relevant law. Before doing so the relevant statutory retention requirements must be considered.

12.2 CREST transactions

Many transactions relating to share registration are now evidenced by electronic instructions for companies whose shares or debentures are capable of being held in CREST, i.e. quoted companies. Indeed, the share register of any company which is a CREST participant is now held in two parts, one for paper certificates and one for electronic holdings in CREST. The electronic part of the register is actually held by the CREST operator rather than the company or its registrar, although the company is still required to keep a shadow copy of this part of the register and to make it available for public inspection. Companies do so by actioning the same instructions for this shadow register as are actioned by the CREST operator. However, as the register held by the CREST operator is the register for the purposes of determining membership, the extent of a company's liabilities in this area are much reduced. Accordingly, the reasons for retaining CREST data will not always be the same as the reasons for retaining background documentation in support of entries made in the register for certificated shares, except where the transaction involves a transfer between the uncertificated and certificated parts of the register. These differences will often enable CREST data to be held for a much shorter period, particularly as the CREST operator is required to maintain an 'adequate record of demateri-alised instructions'.

12.3 Statutory retention requirements

Many of the documents that support entries made in a company's register of members will need to be treated as part of the company's accounting records. These should be kept for a minimum of six years in the case of public companies and three years in the case of private companies (CA ss 221 and 222). These requirements will apply to documents supporting any share transaction which affects an entry in the company's balance sheet, such as a share issue, call for payment, bonus issue, redemption or purchase of own shares but not, for example, a share transfer. Some, but not all, of these transactions may also have tax consequences. Whether or not this is the case, it is normal to assume that any document that forms part of the accounting records should also be retained for tax purposes. Accordingly, it is recommended that the absolute minimum retention period for these types of supporting documents should be six years from the end of the financial year.

The only other relevant statutory requirement relates to contracts for the purchase by a company of its own shares, which must be kept for a minimum of ten years and made available for inspection at its registered office (CA s 164).

12.4 Share issues

When a person subscribes for shares in a company, they enter into a contract with the company. The point at which they obtain enforceable rights under that contract varies depending on who made the offer and whether its acceptance has been notified. In a rights issue, the company makes the offer, which can then be accepted by the person to whom it was made by signing and returning the provisional allotment letter and remitting any payments required. If the offer is renounceable, the person to whom it was made can renounce their rights to subscribe in favour of a third party, who may then accept the offer in their place. On an application for shares, it is the applicant who makes the offer, which may then be accepted or rejected by the company. The contract in this case does not become enforceable until the company has accepted the offer and notified acceptance, e.g. by giving notice of allotment or sending the applicant a share certificate.

In normal circumstances, the limitation period for any contractual disputes regarding the issue of shares would, in England and Wales, be six years, this being the limitation period for actions on an ordinary contract. The fact that share certificates are normally issued under seal has no bearing on the nature of the contract. The seal in this case is merely a device to ensure that the certificate performs its function as a document of title. If, however, the contract to subscribe for shares was executed as a deed (which would be unusual), the limitation period would, of course, be 12 years.

Once a person becomes a member of a company, their relationship with the company is affected by CA, s 14. This provides that a company's memorandum and articles of association bind the company and its members to the same extent as if they respectively had been signed and sealed by each member, and contained covenants on the part of each member to observe all the provisions of the memorandum and articles. Although it is generally agreed that s 14(1) gives rise to a limitation period of 12 years for an action by a company to enforce the provisions of its memorandum or articles against a member, this would not necessarily be true for an action by a member against the company. This is because s 14(1) makes no mention of the company's contract containing covenants or the method by which it is deemed to be executed. Although s 14(2) provides that money payable by a member to the company under the memorandum and articles is a debt due to the company, which in England and Wales it is to be treated as a specialty debt (i.e. one for which the limitation period is 12 years), it makes no such provision regarding debts owed by the company to its members (e.g. unpaid interest or dividends). It has consequently been held that the limitation period for claims by members for unpaid dividends is just six years (see **12.8**).

It should be noted that members have statutory rights to sue the company, its directors and its promoters for any losses suffered as a consequence of the issue of a misleading prospectus or misleading or defective listing particulars. The common law also provides remedies for fraudulent misrepresentation or deceit that may be applicable whether or not a prospectus was issued. In addition, a person to whom a pre-emption offer should be made may, if it is not properly made in accordance with the Act, make a claim against the company or its officers for compensation under s 92, although there is a two-year time limit for bringing such proceedings.

12.5 Rectification

A person who has a contractual right to have their name entered in the register of members can enforce that right by applying to the court for a rectification order against the company (CA s 359). When it makes an order, the court can also award damages.

A person can also apply for a rectification order to have their name removed from the register of members. They might do so on the basis that they never agreed to become a member. This is most likely to occur when a company makes a call on partly-paid shares or a guarantee or unlimited company goes into liquidation. Generally speaking, people tend not to deny that they agreed to become a member if they have been registered as the holder of fully paid shares. However, this possibility cannot be completely discounted. Think how you would feel if you were gifted shares in a company that was a front for a money laundering operation or an unlimited company.

It is hard to say what the limitation period for such an action would be. If one exists, it is unlikely that it would begin to run against the person seeking the order until the company had refused their request to have their name removed from the register. Otherwise, it would be possible to enter someone's name in a register as the holder of unpaid shares and simply wait for the limitation period to expire before making a call on those shares. It is doubtful whether the long-stop limitation period of 20 years in s 352(7) would apply in these circumstances, except perhaps to prevent the person seeking an award of damages.

A company will be able to defeat any attempt to obtain a rectification order in these circumstances if it is able to produce documentary evidence in support of the entry in the register, i.e. a document executed by or on behalf of the person proving that they agreed to become a member or subscribe for the shares. These documents could be crucially important in the case of company with partly-paid shares, guarantee companies and unlimited companies. Accordingly, share issue documents relating to partly-paid shares should probably be retained for as long as there are any outstanding liabilities on those shares. As it is unlikely that a company will need or want to defend such an action in relation to shares that are fully paid, the normal retention period of six years can thereafter be applied. Guarantee companies should probably retain evidence of agreement to become a member for every member for as long as they remain liable under the guarantee, i.e. for at least a year after membership ceases. Unlimited companies should also keep evidence of a person's agreement to become a member until they cease to be a member.

It should finally be noted that in rectification proceedings, a court may refuse to grant an order to remove a person's name from the register if that person has exercised any of the rights or benefits of membership, even though the company may otherwise be unable to prove that they agreed to become a member.

12.6 Share transfers

A company may not normally register a transfer of shares unless it receives a written instrument of transfer (CA s 183). Transfers processed through the CREST system provide the main exception to this rule (see 12.2). If a written transfer is required, the stock transfer form must always be signed by the person transferring the shares. The signature of the person acquiring the shares is only required if the transfer relates to partly-paid shares or shares in an unlimited company. In both these cases, the transfer form will be vitally important from the company's point of view as it may be needed to prove that the person was willing to undertake the outstanding liabilities associated with those shares. On this basis, transfer forms relating to partly-paid shares should probably never be destroyed until all the outstanding liabilities on those shares have been paid in full or, in the case of an unlimited company, until the person ceases to be a member or the company is dissolved.

i Forged transfers

Apart from the circumstances mentioned above, the main reason for keeping stock transfer forms and related documents will be to protect the company against any liabilities it may incur as a consequence of a forged transfer. In law, a forged transfer is a nullity. Accordingly, the original holder is entitled to be restored to the register. This right can be enforced by applying to the court for a rectification order under s 359. When it makes a rectification order, the court can also order the company to pay damages to the true owner, e.g. for lost dividends. This apart, it may not actually cost the company anything to comply with the order. The person who will suffer the greatest loss will be the person into whose name the shares were transferred, which could be the perpetrator of the forgery or, in the case of a market transaction, an innocent third party. The company will not be liable to compensate this innocent third party, although they would normally have a remedy against their broker. If, however, a company issues a share certificate pursuant to a forged transfer, and an innocent third party then buys those shares on the strength of that share certificate, the company will be liable to pay compensation. This is, of course, what often happens when a share transfer has been forged. The person who forged the transfer will normally sell the shares as soon as they get their share certificate. As the company will have an obligation to restore the original holder to the register, it might be necessary to compensate these innocent purchasers in cash, although quoted companies generally purchase shares in the market to restore the true owner to the register and leave the innocent purchaser on the register.

Case law suggests that the limitation period for an action for reinstatement to the register only runs against the true owner from the time that the demand for reinstatement is refused (*Barton v North Staffordshire Ry Co (1888) 38 ChD 458* and *Welch v Bank of England [1955] Ch 508*). Accordingly, it is possible that a company could be required to rectify the register many years after the transfer was registered. It is not clear whether the long-stop limitation period of 20 years in s 352(7) would apply to such proceedings, although it would seem to preclude the true owner from seeking an award of damages against the company after 20 years. The section would almost certainly operate to preclude a company's liability to compensate innocent third parties who subsequently purchased the shares on the strength of share certificates issued by the company. This effectively means that a company will probably have no significant financial liability for a forged transfer that comes to light more than 20 years after registration, and therefore no particular interest thereafter in the retention of stock transfer forms and related documents.

If it is possible for a member to obtain a rectification order 20 or more years after the event, a company may, however, still be expected to be able to produce the relevant stock transfer form. This may, after all, be the only evidence available to the member to show that the transfer was indeed a forgery. This expectation is legitimised to a certain extent by the fact that companies usually take power in their articles to keep instruments of transfer lodged for registration (see, for example, reg 28 of Table A). This is infinitely preferable from the members' point of view because the company might otherwise be required to return the transfer documentation to the person that submitted it for registration (i.e. the forgeror). Nevertheless, it is arguable that if a company exercises its power to keep these documents, it has an obligation or duty to do so for as long as they may be useful, not only to itself but to its members as well. If this is true, it is possible that a member who can prove that they have suffered any loss as a consequence of the company's breach of duty in this regard will be able to sue the company for compensation. Or so the theory goes.

In practice, the chances of a member taking more than 20 years to spot that they have been the victim of a forgery would seem to be slight. And even they did take that long to notice, they might have some difficulty proving their case against the company. If you add to this the fact that the company could argue that the long-stop limitation period of 20 years applies and the fact that the register of members is meant to be *prima facie* evidence, this risk hardly seems worth mentioning. Our purpose in doing so, however, is to draw the attention of readers to the fact that applying the retention period that is recommended in this Guide for stock transfer forms and related documents (i.e. 20 years) could involve some residual risk. Accordingly, any company that is totally risk averse should either insure those risks, retain stock transfer forms for the life of the company or make special provision in its articles to dispose of them earlier (see **12.7**).

When a company receives a transfer for registration, it would seem sensible for it to check that the signature of the person purporting to transfer the shares is genuine. In practice, most listed companies and their registrars do not do so, partly because they may not have anything to check the signature against, but also because checking signatures is a time consuming, expensive and largely fruitless process. Any half decent forgery will normally escape detection. Listed companies can, in any case, rely on the fact that most transfers are submitted for registration by brokers or agents, who are deemed in law to warrant that the transfer is genuine and who will therefore be liable to compensate the company if this proves not to be the case. Listed companies and their registrars still bear some of the risk in these circumstances. The broker may no longer exist when the losses arise or be unable to pay the full amount of any compensation. They may also bear the risk in relation to transfers not submitted by brokers or agents, although they will normally insure at least some of these residual risks.

It is probably sensible, and certainly more viable, for a private companies and an unquoted public company to carry out certain basic checks before registering a transfer of shares. If the member seeking to transfer the shares acquired them in a new issue, the company will probably be able to check the signature on the transfer form against the signature on the application for shares, assuming that member signed it and the company has actually kept it. Where a company has nothing to check the signature on a transfer against, or where its suspicions have been aroused on making any checks, it could try to contact the member to confirm their intentions. Writing a letter indicating that the transfer will be registered within a certain number of days unless the member instructs the company otherwise will not be sufficient for these purposes. If the member fails to respond and the transfer subsequently proves to be a forgery, the company will still be liable for compensation. In these circumstances only the active confirmation of the member would suffice.

12.7 Early disposal of share registration and dividend records

The recommended retention period for stock transfer forms and related documents in the previous edition of this Guide was generally '12 years for the original plus a permanent microfilmed copy'. The recommended retention period in this edition of the Guide has been reduced to 20 years.

It also now states that originals are preferable, but not essential. The new 20-year retention period is thought to be a relatively safe because of the long-stop limitation period of 20 years established by s 352(7) in respect of a company's liabilities for errors and omissions in the administration of its share register. As mentioned previously, however, a company that is totally risk averse might prefer to make special provision in its articles before adopting this recommendation.

Listed companies may also find that it is prudent to make special provision in their articles, although not necessarily for the same reasons. External service registrars tend to treat a retention period of just six years as the norm these days for stock transfer forms. That is not to say that they will not retain documents for longer if requested to do so. However, it is increasingly likely that this service will only come at an extra cost. There is, of course, nothing intrinsically wrong with adopting a retention period of less than 20 years. There are no relevant statutory requirements in this area. However, where a shorter period is applied, someone somewhere must be bearing some risk, no matter how small, of a forgery coming to light after the relevant forms have been destroyed. That person could be the company, its registrar or their respective insurers, depending on the arrangements between the various parties. To make a proper risk assessment, companies that outsource their share registration function need to take into account:

- the retention policies actually applied by their registrars;
- the level of any relevant insurance cover;
- whether that cover would still be effective if relevant documentary evidence is not retained;
- whether the registrars would be liable to indemnify the company in full for any uninsured losses it may incur; or
- whether the contract with the registrars seeks to exclude or limit their liability.

If a company's service contract with its registrars provides for stock transfer forms to be retained for just six years, it will almost certainly be the company that bears the risk. These risks are not as great as they used to be because most large transfers of shares in companies quoted in the UK are now executed through CREST, which provides more certainty as to the validity of the transfer for both companies and their registrars (see **12.2**). In addition, most forgeries will probably come to light long before the six years are up. Nevertheless, the scale of the company's potential liabilities may make the risks difficult to ignore. There are, of course, ways in which these risks can be reduced. One would be to take out a special insurance policy. Another would be to adopt articles which seek to minimise any liabilities that the company might otherwise incur. This would also be in the best interests of the company's registrars if they bear any of the risks involved.

This edition of the Guide recommends that original copies of share registration documents that may be required to provide evidence of execution should be retained. Although a copy could be tendered as evidence in legal proceedings, it would almost certainly not be given the same weight. Indeed, it might be impossible, even for an expert, to say conclusively whether a signature is genuine without the original. It should also be noted that failure to keep the original could invalidate any relevant insurance policy. All of these factors obviously need to be taken into account before making any decision to retain scanned copies instead of the originals. Having said that, there is no reason why a company should not adopt such a policy after making a proper assessment of the risks involved and where they lie. Yet again though, it would probably be prudent for the company to make special provision in its articles before doing so, although this might not eliminate all the risks involved.

If a company suffers any losses as a consequence of a forged transfer, it will obviously have a cause of action against the person who submitted the forged transfer. However, the perpetrator might not be easy to find, and may not be worth suing anyway. Where the transfer was submitted by a broker or agent, it will probably be much easier, and far more profitable, to sue them for breach of their implied warranty. As the name of the broker or agent who submitted the transfer can normally be found on the stock transfer form and the limitation period for such an action would be six years, this is probably the shortest retention period that it would be sensible for any company to apply.

The following wording is provided merely by way of example of the type of article listed companies tend to adopt in this area. It allows the company to dispose of instruments of transfer and other share registration documents after a specified period and seeks to minimise the company's liability for doing so. Although the effect of such a provision has not been tested in the courts, there is no reason to suppose that it would not be effective against the members. Companies should obviously take legal advice before adopting such an article.

(A) The Company shall be entitled to destroy:

    (i) all instruments of transfer of shares which have been registered, and all other documents on the basis of which any entry is made in the register, at any time after the expiration of six years from the date of registration or entry;

    (ii) all dividend mandates, variations or cancellations of dividend mandates, and notifications of change of address at any time after the expiration of two years from the date of recording the matters in such document;

    (iii) all share certificates which have been cancelled at any time after the expiration of one year from the date of the cancellation;

    (iv) all paid dividend warrants and cheques at any time after the expiration of one year from the date of actual payment;

    (v) all proxy appointments which have been used for the purpose of a poll at any time after the expiration of one year from the date of use; and

    (vi) all proxy appointments which have not been used for the purpose of a poll at any time after one month from the end of the meeting to which the proxy appointment relates and at which no poll was demanded.

(B) It shall conclusively be presumed in favour of the Company that:

    (i) every entry in the register purporting to have been made on the basis of an instrument of transfer or other document destroyed in accordance with paragraph (A) above was duly and properly made;

    (ii) every instrument of transfer destroyed in accordance with paragraph (A) above was a valid and effective instrument duly and properly registered;

    (iii) every share certificate destroyed in accordance with paragraph (A) above was a valid and effective certificate duly and properly cancelled; and

    (iv) every other document destroyed in accordance with paragraph (A) above was a valid and effective document in accordance with its recorded particulars in the books or records of the Company,

but:-

    (a) the provisions of this Article apply only to the destruction of a document in good faith and without notice of any claim (regardless of the parties) to which the document might be relevant;

(b) nothing in this Article shall be construed as imposing on the Company any liability in respect of the destruction of any document earlier than the time specified in paragraph (A) above or in any other circumstances which would not attach to the Company in the absence of this Article; and

(c) any reference in this Article to the destruction of any document includes a reference to its disposal in any manner or deletion.

12.8 Dividends and interest payments

The limitation period for actions relating to the payment of dividends is six years, as for actions founded on a simple contract debt under the Limitation Act (*Re Compania de Electricidad de la Provincia de Buenos Aires Ltd [1978] 3 All ER 668*). The decision of Slade J in this case reversed an earlier authority that dividends were a specialty debt which, under s 8(1) of the Limitation Act 1980, would now attract a limitation period of 12 years.

The time limit runs from the declaration of the dividend or, if later, the declared date of payment. However, if the shares are in bearer form and the articles require the share warrant or dividend docket to be presented before payment can be made, no cause of action will arise until they are so presented.

The limitation period for unclaimed interest payments is six years from the due date of payment. A balance sheet entry showing unclaimed dividends or interest payments may amount to an acknowledgment of the debt by the company which may revive the right of action after the limitation period has expired (LA 1980, s 29(5)). Such an acknowledgement must be 'made to the person or to the agent of the person whose title or claim is being acknowledged' (LA 1980, s 30(2)(b)). Accordingly, only a person who can prove receipt of the relevant accounts will be able to take advantage of this provision. A person not entitled to receive a copy or to whom one was sent but not received will not have his debt acknowledged.

Articles often make specific provision for forfeiture of unclaimed dividends. Notwithstanding the *Electricidad* case, reg 108 of Table A provides that any dividend which has remained unclaimed for twelve years after the date when it became due for payment shall, if the directors so resolve, be forfeited and cease to remain owing by the company. Forfeiture after 12 years remains the norm for listed companies, although the provision in the Listing Rules that used to prohibit listed companies from adopting articles making provision for forfeiture less than 12 years after the payment date has now been deleted (former para 17 of Appendix 1 to Chapter 13). Forfeiture under such provisions will

Retention Schedule 2: Share registration and dividends

Record Description	Regulatory retention period and source	Recommended retention period
Registers (see 12.1–12.7)		
1 Register of members	Life of company [CA s 352].	Same.
2 Register of debentures or loan stock holders		Minimum of six year after redemption.
Share issue documentation		
3 Forms of share application	Three–six years [CA s 222].	Minimum of six year or, if later, until share are fully paid.
4 Forms of acceptance	Three–six years [CA s 222].	Minimum of six year or, if later, until share are fully paid.
5 Renounced letters of acceptance and allotment	Three–six years [CA s 222].	Minimum of six year or, if later, until share are fully paid.
6 Renounced share certificates	Three–six years [CA s 222].	Minimum of six year or, if later, until share are fully paid.
Share transfers and related documentation		
7 Share and stock transfer forms		20 years unless special powers taken in articles.

extinguish any right of action for unclaimed dividends, including any extension under the acknowledgement rules. It will be a matter of construction of the relevant articles whether, in the absence of any acknowledgement, such articles operate to extend the limitation period established in the *Electricidad* case. In view of the potential uncertainty surrounding this area, companies would be well-advised to retain schedules relating to unclaimed dividends until such time as they are forfeited in accordance with the articles.

Form in which to be kept	Reasons and remarks
In any form (including electronic) [CA, ss 722 and 723].	CA, s 352(6) permits records to be removed from the register 20 years after membership ceases.
In any form (including electronic) [CA ss 722 and 723].	Limitation/Best Practice.
Originals are preferable for evidential reasons.	See **12.3–12.5**, particularly regarding shares in an unlimited company.
Originals are preferable for evidential reasons.	See **12.3–12.5**, particularly regarding shares in an unlimited company.
Originals are preferable for evidential reasons.	See **12.3–12.5**, particularly regarding shares in an unlimited company.
Originals are preferable for evidential reasons.	See **12.3–12.5**, particularly regarding shares in an unlimited company.
Originals are preferable for evidential reasons.	See **12.6** and **12.7**.

Retention Schedule 2: Share registration and dividends – *continued*

Record Description	Regulatory retention period and source	Recommended retention period
8 Request for rectification of transferee details		20 years unless special powers taken in articles.
9 Requests for designating or redesignating accounts		20 years after request unless special powers taken in articles.
10 Letters of request		20 years after request unless special powers taken in articles.
11 Letters of administration and documents of probate		20 years unless special powers taken in articles.
12 Forms of conversion		20 years after date of conversion unless special powers taken in articles.
13 Redemption discharge forms or endorsed certificates		20 years after date of redemption unless special powers taken in articles.
14 Letters of indemnity for lost certificates		Permanently.
15 Cancelled share/stock certificates		One year from the date of registration of transfer.
16 Talisman bought/sold transfers		20 years unless special powers taken in articles.
17 No sub-sale declaration forms		20 years unless special powers taken in articles.

Form in which to be kept	Reasons and remarks
Originals are preferable for evidential reasons.	See **12.6** and **12.7**.
Originals are preferable for evidential reasons.	See **12.6** and **12.7**.
Originals are preferable for evidential reasons.	See **12.6** and **12.7**.
Copy, as originals, if submitted, will normally be returned.	See **12.6** and **12.7**.
Originals are preferable for evidential reasons.	See **12.6** and **12.7**.
Originals are preferable for evidential reasons.	See **12.6** and **12.7**.
Originals are preferable for evidential reasons.	Best Practice.
Original.	Best Practice.
Originals are preferable for evidential reasons.	See **12.6** and **12.7**. Although the Talisman system has been replaced by CREST, registrars may still hold historical records.
Originals are preferable for evidential reasons.	See **12.6** and **12.7**.

Retention Schedule 2: Share registration and dividends – *continued*

Record Description	Regulatory retention period and source	Recommended retention period
Other share registration documents		
18 Notification of change of address		Two years.
19 Copy of evidence submitted in support of a change of name, e.g. deed poll, marriage certificate, certificate of incorporation on change of name		20 years.
20 Contract for the purchase of own shares or, if not in writing, a memorandum of its terms	10 years from date of purchase [CA s 169].	Same.
21 Powers of attorney		12 years after ceasing to be valid.
22 Stop notices and other court orders		Until order no longer valid but up to 20 years where order provides evidence of the reason for any action taken.
23 Trust deed securing issue of debentures or loan stock		12 years after stock has been fully redeemed.
Dividends and interest payments (see 12.8)		
24 Dividend and interest payment lists	Three–six years, [CA s 222].	Same.
25 Paid dividend and interest warrants	Three–six years, [CA s 222].	Six years after date of payment.
26 Dividend and interest mandates		Six years after ceasing to be valid.

Form in which to be kept	Reasons and remarks
As evidence of execution is primary reason for retention, original is preferable.	Best Practice.
Copy as original will normally be returned.	Limitation/Best Practice (but see **12.7**).
If contract is in writing, original must be kept.	Statutory.
Copy as original is normally returned.	Limitation/Best Practice (but see **12.7**).
Any.	Limitation/Best Practice.
Original.	Limitation/Best Practice.

Any.	(Before disposal, an extract of outstanding warrants should be made).
Any.	Limitation (but see **12.7**).
Any, although originals may be preferable for evidential reasons.	Limitation period suggests six years but standard practice of registrars may be less.

13 Meetings and minutes

13.1 Minutes

Companies must keep minutes of general meetings and of meetings of directors (CA 1985, s 382). This will include all meetings of shareholders, including class meetings, and all meetings of directors, including any committee of directors. Section 382 also requires minutes to be kept of meetings of 'managers'. A manager is probably someone who exercises the power of a director but is not actually appointed as such. The best example would be the chief executive of a charity, who will not normally be a member of the main board. If there are two or more such persons who have to exercise their power collectively, the Act probably requires minutes of their meetings to be kept.

Minutes may be kept in a bound book or in any other manner provided that adequate measures are taken to guard against falsification and to facilitate their discovery (s 722). In theory, minutes may be kept on computer (s 723). However, minutes will be evidence of the proceedings only if they are signed by the chairman of the meeting or the chairman of the next meeting. Although it is currently possible for an individual to apply a unique electronic signature to a computer file that would probably be acceptable in legal proceedings, this would mean that the technology to decrypt the signature would have to be retained for the life of the company. Not only that, the personal signature of the chairman would have to be known by the company or be capable of being made known to it in the event of his death or incapacity. Finally, what may be an unbreakable code today, may become readily decipherable in a few years time. On the whole, it is probably still best to keep original signed copies of the minutes in a bound or loose-leaf minute book.

13.2 Other meetings documentation

If proper detailed minutes are drafted, there should not be any great need to keep agenda papers and supporting documents. Board agenda papers will undoubtedly have commercial value for a number of years. However, the fact that the papers are normally kept for lengthy periods, should not distract company secretaries from seeking to avoid drafting minutes which require frequent reference to be made to external documents for a full understanding. If such references are made, the documents will need to be kept for the life of the company in the same way as the minutes themselves. Indeed, it is arguable that the documents should themselves be entered in the minute book.

13.3 Sealing and directors' interests registers

If a register is used to record transactions which the board or a board committee has approved for sealing, and the minutes of the relevant meetings simply refer to the entry numbers in the register which were approved, then that register must also be treated in the same manner as the minutes. The same will be true of any register kept to record directors' declarations of interests in transactions where these are not recorded in full in the minutes of board meetings.

Retention Schedule 3: Meetings and minutes

Record Description	Regulatory retention period and source	Recommended retention period
1 Agenda papers		Minimum of seven years. Life for any paper which is necessary in order to understand the minutes.
2 Board minutes (signed copy)	Life of company: [CA, s 382].	Same.
3 Board committee minutes (signed copy)	Life of company: [CA, s 382].	Same.
4 Written resolutions of the board	Life of company: [CA, s 382].	Same.
5 Attendance record		If required by articles (e.g. reg 86 of 1948 Table A). Life of company.
6 Register of directors' declarations of interest	Life of company: [CA, ss 317 and 382].	Same.
7 Sealing register	Life of company: [CA, s 382].	Life where articles require board (or board committee) to approve sealing of documents and relevant minutes refer to entries in sealing register.

Form in which to be kept	Reasons and remarks
	Limitation/commercial. It is not good practice to draft minutes that require agenda papers to be kept in this manner.
In any form (including electronic) [CA, ss 722 and 723], although minute books are usually kept in paper form for evidential reasons.	Signed originals should be entered in a minute book.
In any form (including electronic) [CA, ss 722 and 723], although minute books are usually kept in paper form for evidential reasons.	Signed originals should be entered in a minute book.
In any form (including electronic) [CA, ss 722 and 723], although minute books are usually kept in paper form for evidential reasons.	Record of written resolution (and/or signed originals) should be entered in minute book. If signed originals not entered, they should be kept for at least six years.
As required by articles.	If separate record not required by articles, the list of attendees in the minutes will suffice.
In any form (including electronic) [CA, ss 722 and 723].	Details of directors' declarations should either be recorded in the minutes or in a register. If entered in a register, it must be treated as a subset of the minutes.
In any form (including electronic) [CA, ss 722 and 723].	If full details of documents approved for sealing are included in the minutes, these reasons do not apply. However, it will still be good practice to keep any register for at least 12 years after the date of the last entry.

Retention Schedule 3: Meetings and minutes – *continued*

Record Description	Regulatory retention period and source	Recommended retention period
Shareholder Meetings		
8 Notices of general and class meetings (signed copy)		12 years minimum. Life if notice is necessary to understand the minutes.
9 Circulars to shareholders (master copy)		12 years minimum. Life if circular is necessary to understand the minutes.
10 Certificate of posting of notices		Two years minimum suggested.
11 Minutes of general and class meetings	Life of company: [CA, s 382].	Same.
12 Record of statutory written resolutions of company	Life of company: [CA, s 382].	Same.
13 Written record of decision of sole member	Life of company: [CA, s 382B].	Same.
14 Proxy forms – no poll demanded		One month after meeting.

Form in which to be kept	Reasons and remarks
Original preferable.	Business needs/ Evidence/In case of challenge to validity of meeting and/or resolutions by virtue of defective notice.
Original preferable.	Same reason as above (circular deemed to be part of the notice).
Original preferable.	The likelihood of anyone challenging the validity of a meeting on the grounds of lack of notice is slim, and any such challenge will normally be initiated fairly soon after the meeting.
In any form (including electronic) [CA, ss 722 and 723], although minute books are usually kept in paper form for evidential reasons.	Signed originals should be entered in minute book.
In any form (including electronic) [CA, ss 722 and 723], although minute books are usually kept in paper form for evidential reasons.	Statutory – Record of resolution (and of signatures) must be entered in the minute book and signed by a director or the secretary. Signed originals need not be included but it is good practice to retain them for at least 12 years.
In any form (including electronic) [CA, ss 722 and 723], although minute books are usually kept in paper form for evidential reasons.	Statutory – Record should be entered in minute book.
Proxies may have been submitted in paper or electronic form.	Best Practice.

Retention Schedule 3: Meetings and minutes – *continued*

Record Description	Regulatory retention period and source	Recommended retention period
15 Proxy forms/polling cards – poll demanded		One year after meeting.
16 Proxy forms used at meetings convened by court		At direction of court or one year after court supervision.

Form in which to be kept	Reasons and remarks
Proxy forms would be retained in the format in which they were submitted. Polling cards would be in paper form.	Best Practice.
Retained in form in which they are submitted.	

14 Accounting and tax records

14.1 Accounting records

For most businesses, accounting records are likely to pose one of the greatest problems in terms of storage. Section 222(5) of the Companies Act 1985 states that accounting records must be retained:

- in the case of a public company, for a minimum of six years from the date they were made; and
- in the case of a private company, for a minimum of three years from the date they were made.

Any director or officer of a company who fails to take all reasonable steps for securing compliance with s 222(5), or intentionally causes any default by the company thereof, is guilty of an offence and liable to imprisonment (two years maximum) or a fine (£5,000 maximum) or both.

The Companies Act requirements are only a minimum and other factors need be taken into account. For example, some accounting records also need to be retained for tax purposes (see below). This will be of particular relevance to private companies as the rules for tax purposes are more onerous than s 222. In view of these requirements, the potential liabilities of directors and officers and the commercial value of accounting records, it is usual to retain the accounting ledgers (and the supporting documentation) for longer than the statutory minimum. Any recommendation in this regard will be somewhat arbitrary and businesses should determine their own rules according to their own needs. However, a retention period of between six and seven years would generally seem to be the norm.

Accounting entries may be kept 'in a non-legible form', e.g. on computer, as long as they are capable of being reproduced in a legible form (s 723). Where they are stored on computer, it follows that the hardware and software required to retrieve them must also be retained for the relevant period specified in s 222(5).

It will normally be possible to destroy original copies of invoices, receipts and other supporting documents if a microfilm or computerised image is made (see further below for specific rules for tax and VAT purposes). However many auditors still prefer to work from the original documents and companies are strongly advised to consult them before implementing a document imaging or microfilm programme for accounting records and vouchers.

Section 221 of the Companies Act 1985 requires accounting records to be kept which are sufficient to show and explain a company's transactions and which enable its directors to prepare accounts that give a true and fair view of the company's affairs. Accounting records must *in particular* contain:

- entries from day-to-day of all sums of money received and expended by the company, and the matters for which receipt and expenditure takes place;
- a record of the company's assets and liabilities;
- if the business involves dealing in goods:
  - statements of stock held by the company at the end of each financial year and any statements of stocktaking from which any such statement has been prepared, and
  - except in the case of goods sold by way of ordinary retail trade, statements of all goods sold and purchased, showing sufficient detail to enable the goods, the buyers and the sellers to be identified.

Companies are required to retain accounting ledgers and sufficient documentary evidence to explain the entries made in those accounting ledgers for the specified period. The table below lists the main records that must be retained. The list is not exhaustive. When deciding whether other accounting documents should be retained in accordance with the Act, the determining factor will be whether they are necessary to explain the company's transactions and prepare the final accounts.

i Main accounting records required to be kept under the Companies Act 1985

Ledgers	*Supporting documents*
Cash book	Purchase invoices and credit notes
Purchase ledger	Copy sales invoices and credit notes
Sales ledger	Journal vouchers
Asset registers	Consignment notes

Ledgers	*Supporting documents*
Nominal and private ledgers	Stock records
Journal ledgers	Petty cash vouchers
Individual debtors accounts	Bank statements and reconciliations
End of year stock records	Loan agreements
	Rental and hire purchase agreements
	Indemnities and guarantees
	Share and debenture issue documentation.

In March 1992, the Institute of Chartered Accountants in England and Wales issued a statement, which was settled in consultation with counsel, on the obligation to keep accounting records under CA 1985. This statement said:

'[t]he accounting records should comprise an orderly, classified collection of information capable of timely retrieval, containing details of the company's transactions, assets and liabilities. An unorganised collection of vouchers and documents will not suffice: whatever the physical form of records, the information should be so organised as to enable a trial balance to be constructed. If, for example the information is held in a computer database as a subset of a set of wider information, the software should be capable of retrieving the appropriate data.'

14.2 Report and accounts

Most companies get several copies of the annual report and accounts signed by the relevant signatories. One of those signed copies must be filed at Companies House within the period for delivery (10 months after the year end for private companies and seven months for public companies). Other regulators (e.g. the Financial Services Authority for regulated businesses) may also require a signed copy. If the accounts were audited, the auditors will usually request a signed copy for themselves. Whatever the number required for external purposes, most companies will also produce at least one additional signed copy for themselves. Whilst this is plainly sensible as a backup in case any of the copies sent to Companies House and other regulators do not arrive at their destination, it is difficult to point to any law or regulation which requires a company to keep a signed copy itself. For example, if the accounts sent to Companies House did get lost in the post and the company found it necessary to use its own signed copy to comply with its filing obligations, it is doubtful whether it would be necessary to get another copy signed for retention.

Customs & Excise and the Inland Revenue both expect a copy of the accounts to be retained for at least six years after the year end, and possibly longer if the a final assessment has not been agreed for that year. However, it is doubtful whether either would insist that it should be an original signed copy.

Should a signed copy of the accounts be required for inspection or to be tendered as evidence in legal proceedings, it would be possible to certify that the copy tendered is a true copy. It is also possible for a company to obtain a certified copy of its accounts from Companies House.

Companies will probably need to keep several spare copies of the last published accounts to satisfy requests for copies made by members or debenture holders pursuant to CA 1985, s 239. Copies supplied for these purposes need not, of course, be signed originals. A company can comply with its obligations under s 239 by providing a copy using electronic communication, as long as the person who made the request agrees (CA 1985, s 239(2A)).

Bearing all these issues in mind, it is recommended that:

- one copy of a company's report and accounts (preferably, but not necessarily, a signed copy) should be kept with the company's other statutory books and records for the life of the company;
- an unsigned copy of the accounts should be kept with the tax records and destroyed when the necessary retention period for those documents has expired;
- sufficient copies should be kept until the next accounts are published to comply with requests from members and debenture holders under CA 1985, s 239;
- these and any other copies may be destroyed when they no longer serve any commercial purpose.

It is even harder to find any legal reason for retaining copies of interim or quarterly reports, but these will not normally have been filed at Companies House.

14.3 Value Added Tax (VAT)

Organisations which are registered for VAT are required to keep such records, accounts and related documents as the Commissioners may require for six years, VAT Act 1994, s 58 and Sch 11, para 6(3). Records must be kept of all operations which affect the amount of VAT a business has to pay or can reclaim. This includes:

- every supply of goods or services received on which VAT is charged;
- services listed in s 31 received from abroad;
- every EC acquisition, importation or removal from warehouse;
- all the supplies made by the business (including any zero-rated or exempt supplies);
- any goods exported;
- any gifts or loans of goods;
- any taxable self-supplies – for example, cars;
- any goods acquired or produced in the course of business which are put to private or other non-business use;
- corrections to accounts;
- amended VAT invoices;
- any credits allowed or received; and
- any capital item acquired or created for use in the business.

Documents and records which should be retained for VAT purposes include:

- annual accounts, including profit and loss accounts;
- bank statements and paying-in slips;
- cash books and other account books;
- credit or debit notes you issue or receive;
- documentation relating to dispatches/acquisitions of goods to/from EC Member States;
- documents or certificates supporting special VAT treatment such as relief on supplies to visiting forces or zero-rating by certificate;
- import and export documents;
- orders and delivery notes;
- purchase and sales books;
- purchase invoices and copy sales invoices;
- records of daily takings such as till rolls;
- relevant business correspondence; and
- VAT account.

If these requirements cause storage problems or involve undue expense or cause other difficulties, an application can be made to Customs & Excise for permission to keep some records for a shorter period. On no account should records be destroyed without the agreement of Customs & Excise.

VAT records may be kept on microfilm or microfiche, provided copies can be easily produced and there are adequate facilities for allowing a Customs & Excise officer to view them when required. Before transferring records to microfilm or microfiche, clearance should be obtained from the relevant local VAT office which may require the old and new systems to be operated side by side for a limited period. Customs & Excise has power to refuse or withdraw approval for the use of microfilm or microfiche if its requirements are not met.

VAT records may also be kept on a computer, for example, on magnetic tape, disk etc, provided again that they can be readily converted into a satisfactory legible form and made available to Customs & Excise on request. Any business which decides to use a computer or the services of a computer bureau for VAT accounting should first notify its local VAT office. Where a computer bureau is used, the taxpayer is responsible for arranging for the bureau to make VAT records available to Customs & Excise when it wishes to see them. Customs & Excise also has power to refuse or withdraw approval for the use of computer media if its requirements cannot be met.

Customs & Excise has agreed a statement of good practice for VAT accounting software with the Business and Accounting Software Developers Association (BASDA). Details of packages that have been independently certified as complying with the statement of good practice, are available from: BASDA, 530 Linen Hall, 162–168 Regent Street, London W1R 5TB (www.basda.org)

14.4 Inland Revenue

A person or a business can be required to deliver or make available for inspection all documents *in their possession* which might reasonably be expected to contain information relevant to any tax liability under investigation (TMA 1970, s 20). This will include any books, accounts and any other documents or records.

The period for which tax documents must be held differs according to the type of tax chargeable and the person liable to pay it. The rules for individuals and unincorporated businesses are contained in s 12 of the TMA 1970. The rules for corporation tax records are contained in Sch 18 of FA 1998 (see **14.5** below). As a general rule, records must be kept for a certain minimum period, usually related to the normal period for making an assessment. Records may however need to be kept longer in certain circumstances (see **14.8**). Where the Revenue has reasonable grounds to believe that tax has been lost as a result of fraud, wilful default or negligence, the period for making an assessment may be extended by a further six years in the case of negligence, and indefinitely in the case of fraud or wilful default (TMA 1970, ss 36–39).

For businesses that are not limited companies, records must normally be retained for five years from the 31 January following the tax year for which the tax return is made. For example, for the 2003 tax return sent to the business on 6 April 2003, to be completed by 31 January 2004, records must be retained until at least 31 January 2009.

Individuals not carrying on a business who are required to complete a tax return will normally have to retain their records for at least 12 months from the end of the tax year to which they relate. For example, for the 2003 tax return issued on 6 April 2003, records will have to be kept until at least 31 January 2005.

14.5 Corporation tax self-assessment

The obligations relating to the retention of records for the purposes of corporation tax self-assessment are contained in FA 1998, Sch 18, paras 21–23. A company must keep sufficient records to enable it to deliver a correct and complete tax return. Subject to the exceptions in **14.8**, the records must be preserved for six years from the end of the period for which the company may be required to deliver a company tax return

The records required to be kept and preserved include records of:

- all receipts and expenses in the course of the company's activities, and the matters for which the receipts and expenses arise;
- in the case of a trade involving dealing in goods, all sales and purchases made in the course of the trade; and
- all supporting documents relating to the items mentioned above (including accounts, books, deeds, contracts, vouchers and receipts).

Companies may satisfy the duty to preserve records for these purposes by preserving the information contained in them (FA 1998, Sch 18, para 22). This means that, subject to certain exceptions (see **14.6**), all tax records and related vouchers can be kept in non-paper form for tax purposes, although a company's auditors may still prefer original vouchers to be kept until they have completed their annual audit.

The Inland Revenue can impose a penalty of up to £3,000 for failure to comply with the requirements to keep records (FA 1998, Sch 18, para 23 and TMA 1970, s 12B(5)). In practice, these penalties only tend to be used in more serious cases, for example, where records have been destroyed deliberately to obstruct an enquiry into the company's tax affairs, or if the company has a history of serious failure to keep records.

14.6 Form in which tax records must be kept

Section 12 of the Taxes Management Act (for unincorporated businesses and individuals) and Sch 18 of FA 1998 (for companies) both provide that the duty to preserve records may be discharged by the preservation of the information contained in them; and where information is so preserved a copy of any document forming part of the records shall be admissible in evidence in any proceedings before the Commissioners to the same extent as the records themselves.

Both also make provision for the following exceptions, which will still need to be kept in paper form where they are received in that form:

- any statement in writing showing the amount of qualifying distribution and tax credit for the purposes of s 234(1) of ICTA 1988;
- any statement in writing showing gross amount, tax deducted and actual amount paid, in certain cases where payments are made under deduction of tax for the purposes of s 352(1) of ICTA 1988;
- any certificate or other record (however described) required by regulations under s 566(1) of ICTA 1988 to be given to a sub-contractor on the making of a payment to which s 559 of that Act applies (deductions on account of tax);
- any record relating to an amount of tax paid under the law of a territory outside the UK, or which would have been so payable but for a relief to which s 788(5) of ICTA 1988 applies (relief for promoting development or contemplated by double taxation arrangements).

It is now possible to elect to receive electronic versions of dividend tax vouchers and statements of the deduction of tax, i.e. the first two categories in the exceptions listed above, as long as the person required to provide the information offers this as an option (see **14.7** below). Where a person opts to receive the statements in electronic form, the electronic file, which must be sent in a form that is capable of being printed but not altered, can be retained for tax purposes and, if necessary, printed.

14.7 Electronic Certificates of Deduction of Tax and Tax Credit

The Income and Corporation Taxes (Electronic Certificates of Deduction of Tax and Tax Credit) Regulations 2003 (SI/2003/3143), which came into force on 1 January 2004 authorise the electronic delivery of certain documents, including:

- information about distributions required under s 234 of ICTA 1988 (e.g. dividend tax vouchers);
- a statement of the deduction of tax, to be given under s 352 of ICTA 1988, and a request for such a statement;
- certain documents required or authorised to be furnished in connection with manufactured dividends.

In each case electronic delivery is authorised only if the:

- sender of the information has previously notified the recipient that he intends to use electronic communications for the particular purpose;
- recipient has consented to electronic delivery of information by the sender and that consent has not been withdrawn;
- electronic format used is designed to prevent alteration of what is delivered, but nonetheless permits a copy of what is delivered to be printed or kept in electronic format.

Electronic delivery includes making the document on a website, and notifying the intended recipient of that fact together with the address of the website and the place on the website at which, and the manner in which, the document may be accessed.

14.8 Circumstances in which tax records have to be kept for longer than usual

Individuals, companies, partnerships and other businesses will need to keep their tax records for longer than the usual minimum in the following circumstances:

- If there is any enquiry into the tax return that has not been completed by the date for which records normally have to be retained, the records for that period must be retained by you until that enquiry is completed.

- Where no enquiry has been started, but the statutory period for starting the enquiry has not been reached by the date for which records normally have to be retained (usually because the tax return has been sent back late). In this case the records must be retained by until the latest date for starting an enquiry has passed or the date such an enquiry is completed, if this is later.

- The date on which the Revenue requests a tax return is after the date to which records normally have to be kept. In that case the records in existence at the date you are requested to complete the tax return must be retained until the latest date for starting an enquiry has passed or, if later, the date such an enquiry is completed.

14.9 PAYE and payroll records

An employer must keep all PAYE records which are not required to be sent to the Inland Revenue for not less than three years after the end of the tax year to which they relate (Income Tax (Pay As You Earn) Regulations 2003 (SI/2003/2682), reg 97). If requested by the Revenue, the employer must produce the records for inspection either at the place in the UK at which the PAYE records are normally kept or, if there is no such place, the employer's principal place of business in the UK.

'PAYE records' are defined in reg 97(2) of the Regulations as:

- all wages sheets, deductions working sheets, documents completed under regulation 46 (Form P46) (other than those which the employer has sent to the Inland Revenue), and other documents and records relating to —
  - the calculation of the PAYE income of the employees,
  - relevant payments to the employees, or
  - the deduction of tax from, or accounting for tax in respect of, such payments, and
- all documents and records relating to any information which an employer is required to provide to the Inland Revenue under reg 85 (Forms P9D and P11D).

The 2003 Regulations referred to above replaced the Income Tax (Employments) Regulations 1993 (SI 1993/744) with effect from 1 April

2004. The 1993 Regulations also required records relating to the calculation of pay to be retained for at least three years after the end of the year to which they relate.

Under the TMA 1970, the Inland Revenue can require an employer to provide a return relating to payments made to employees for up to five years after the 31 January following the year of assessment (s 15). The return may require information on payments made to each employee, including expenses, payments made on the employee's behalf, payments

Retention Schedule 4: Accounting and tax records

Record Description	Regulatory retention period and source	Recommended retention period
1 Accounting records to comply with CA, s 221	Ltd – Three years from date of which they are made: [CA, s 222(5)(a)].	Six years from year end.
	Plc – Six years from date on which they are made: [CA, s 222(5)(b)].	Six years from year end.
2 Report and accounts – signed copy – unsigned copies	Six years: VATA Act 1984, Sch 11.	At least one copy (not necessarily a signed copy) should be kept for the life of the company/business.
3 Interim report and accounts		At least one copy for the life of the company.
4 Budgets and periodic internal financial reports		Six years

rendered in connection with the trade or business and other benefits in kind.

Payroll records also form part of the statutory accounting records and must be kept for general tax purposes as evidence of deductible expenses. As the retention period for these purposes will usually be a minimum of five or six years (depending on the nature of the business), it may be difficult to identify PAYE records that can be destroyed after the three-year period.

Form in which to be kept	Reasons and remarks
In any form (including electronic) [CA, ss 722 and 723].	Most companies will need to keep accounting records for a minimum of six years for tax purposes (see **14.1**).
It is preferable if the copy kept for tax purposes is the signed copy.	Tax/Evidence/Business.
Multiple unsigned copies may be needed to satisfy the demands of members and denture holders in the first year.	To comply with CA requirements.
Preferably an original signed copy.	Evidence/Business (See **14.2**.)
Any.	Evidence/Best Practice/Internal Control.

Retention Schedule 4: Accounting and tax records – *continued*

Record Description	Regulatory retention period and source	Recommended retention period
5 VAT records	Six years: VATA, Sch 11.	
6 Self-assessment records for businesses not subject to corporation tax	Five years from the 31 January following the tax year for which the tax return is made: [TMA 1970, s 12(2)(a)].	Same.
7 Self-assessment tax records of individuals not carrying on a business who are required to complete a tax return	12 months from 31 January next following the year of assessment or, if return delivered late, the quarter day next following the first anniversary of the day the return was delivered: [TMA 1970, s 12(2)(b)].	
8 Corporation tax self-assessment records	Six years from the end of the assessment period: FA 1998, Sch 18, paras 21–23.	Seven years from year end.
9 PAYE records (post-April 2004)	Not less than three years after the end of the tax year to which they relate [Income Tax (Pay As You Earn) Regulations 2003, reg 97].	

Form in which to be kept	Reasons and remarks
Any form for the purposes of Customs & Excise (see **14.3** but original vouchers may be required for audit purposes.	See **14.3**.
Records and vouchers kept for tax purposes may be kept in any form, subject to certain exceptions (see **14.6**). [TMA 1970, s 12(4)]. Original vouchers may be required for audit purposes.	See further **14.4**.
Records and vouchers kept for tax purposes may be kept in any form, subject to certain exceptions (see **14.6**) [TMA 1970, s 12(4)]. Original vouchers may be required for audit purposes.	See **14.4**. (Quarter days for these purposes are 31 January, 30 April, 31 July and 31 October).
Records and vouchers kept for tax purposes may be kept in any form, subject to certain exceptions (see **14.6**). [FA 1998, Sch 18, para 22]. Original vouchers may be required for audit purposes.	See **14.5**.
In any form [implied by Income Tax (Pay As You Earn) Regulations 2003, reg 97(7)].	See further **14.9**. Reg 97 does not apply to documents that must be sent to the Inland Revenue under the Income Tax (Pay As You Earn) Regulations 2003.

Retention Schedule 4: Accounting and tax records – *continued*

Record Description	Regulatory retention period and source	Recommended retention period
Charitable and political donations		
10 Deeds of covenant (donee)	Six years after last payment.	Six years after last payment due but up to 12 years if any payments are still outstanding or there is any dispute regarding the deed
11 Gift aid forms	As per usual tax requirements for charity concerned (e.g. for a charitable company, six years from end of tax year in which the last payment under the declaration was made).	
12 Documents evidencing donations made to charitable and political organisations	Ltd – Three years Plc – Six years: [CA, s 221].	Six years.
Banking records		
13 Cheques, bills of exchange and other negotiable instruments	Ltd – Three years Plc – six years: [CA, s 221].	Six years.
14 Paying-in counterfoils	Ltd – Three years Plc – six years: [CA, s 221].	Six years.
15 Bank statements and reconciliations	Ltd – Three years Plc – six years: [CA, s 221].	Six years.
16 Instructions to banks	Six years after ceasing to be effective.	

Form in which to be kept	Reasons and remarks
Originals.	Tax/Limitation.
Originals or scanned or microfilmed copies [FA 2000, s 39].	Declarations continue in force until revoked or cancelled.
	Tax/Best Practice.
Originals.	Limitation.
Originals.	Limitation.
Any.	Limitation.
Any.	Evidence/Limitation.

15 Employment and pension records

15.1 Employment records

Retention requirements for payroll records are governed principally by accounting and tax rules (see **14.9**). Under the Working Time Regulations 1998 (SI/1998/183) most employers must keep for two years:

- sufficient records to show compliance with the relevant weekly working time and night work limits;
- an up-to-date record of workers who have agreed to work more than 48 hours a week;
- records of health assessments for night workers, and the result of any assessment.

Retention periods for the vast majority of personnel records must be determined according to business need. It should be noted, however, that the Data Protection Act, requires that personal data shall not be kept for longer than is necessary for a particular purpose. The Information Commission has issued a four part code on the application of this principle (*The Employment Practices Data Protection Code* – EPDP Code). The Code deals with:

- Part 1: Recruitment and selection (see below)
- Part 2: Employment records
- Part 3: Monitoring at work
- Part 4: Information about workers' health.

Part 2 of the Code recommends that retention periods for employment records must be based on business need and should take into account any professional guidelines and any relevant statutory requirements. When establishing retention periods employers should:

- make any data about workers and former workers anonymous where practical;
- bear in mind that information should not be retained simply on the basis that 'it might come in useful one day' without any clear view of when or why;
- establish how often particular categories of information are actually accessed after, say, two, three, four or five years;

- adopt a 'risk analysis' approach to retention by considering what realistically would be the consequences for your business, for workers and former workers and for others, should information that is accessed only very occasionally be no longer available;
- base any decision to retain a record on the principle of proportionality. For example, records about a very large number of workers should not be retained for a lengthy period on the off-chance that one of them might at some point question some aspect of his or her employment;
- treat items of information individually or in logical groupings. Do not decide to retain all the information in a record simply because there is a need to retain some of it;
- ensure that records are not kept beyond the standard retention time unless there is a business justification for doing so. With a computerised system this might be facilitated by the automated deletion or automatic flagging of information that is due for deletion. With paper files this is likely to involve the occasional 'weeding' of expired information, perhaps annually for current workers. As far as possible, structure systems to facilitate the retention policy. Make sure that items of information with significantly different retention periods are not recorded on the same piece of paper;
- if records are maintained for management analysis, for example, to check the average period for which various grades of staff remain employed with a company, delete the information which enables particular individuals to be identified;
- if the holding of any information on criminal convictions of workers is justified, ensure that the information is deleted once the conviction is 'spent' under the Rehabilitation of Offenders Act 1974. For example, an employer might have a valid business reason for keeping information about the driving convictions of those who are employed to drive the employer's vehicles. However it is difficult to see any justification for retaining this information once the convictions become 'spent' under the provisions of the Act. In exceptional circumstances which involve jobs covered by the Exceptions Order to this Act there might be a business need that justifies the continued retention of 'spent' convictions. Information about a relevant criminal conviction of a worker who was employed to work with children and was dismissed because of the

conviction may need to be retained. This would be held to ensure the worker is not re-employed in a similar role;

- ensure that records which are to be disposed of are securely and effectively destroyed. Take particular care to ensure that when computer records are deleted they are actually removed from the system. Copies of such records that might have been retained within the system, perhaps on a separate server, or as paper print-outs should be identified and also removed. Establish secure arrangements for the disposal of paper records containing sensitive or confidential information about workers, for example by having them shredded on-site or by a reputable contractor. Do not sell computer equipment unless you are certain that any employment records have been completely removed. Simple 'deletion' will not necessarily achieve this.

15.2 Recruitment records

Recruitment agencies have some legal obligations to retain records under the Employment Agencies Act 1973. That apart, the main reason for keeping recruitment records will probably be to defend against allegations of discrimination in the recruitment process. Actions under discrimination legislation must generally be brought within three months, although tribunals can allow cases to proceed out of time in exceptional circumstances. Retention and use of recruitment records for other purposes may constitute a breach of the Data Protection Act which requires that the personal data in a record shall not be kept for longer than is necessary for a particular purpose or purposes. According to the *Employment Practices Data Protection Code Part 1: Recruitment and Selection (March 2002)*, retention periods should be based on business need and take into account any relevant professional guidelines. The Code also states that 'the possibility that an individual may bring a legal action does not automatically justify the indefinite retention of all records relating to workers. A policy based on risk-analysis principles should be established.'

The Code establishes the following benchmarks for employers in relation to recruitment records.

Establish and adhere to retention periods for recruitment records that are based on a clear business need. Note: Employers should consider the possibility that some business needs might be satisfied by using anonymous, rather than identifiable, records. For example, if the organisation wishes to compare the success of various recruitment campaigns, this could be achieved by using anonymous records

Destroy information obtained by a vetting exercise as soon as possible, or in any case within six months. A record of the result of vetting or verification can be retained. This is consistent with the Criminal Records Bureau Code of Conduct. However, where there is a legal obligation to retain specified information for longer than six months, this must be respected.

Consider carefully which information contained on an application form is to be transferred to the worker's employment record. Delete information irrelevant to on-going employment.

Delete information about criminal convictions collected in the course of the recruitment process once it has been verified through a Criminal Records Bureau disclosure, unless in exceptional circumstances the information is clearly relevant to the on-going employment relationship. A note may be kept showing that a check was completed and the results of the findings.

Advise unsuccessful applicants that their names will be kept on file for future vacancies (if appropriate) and give them the opportunity to have their details removed from the file.

Ensure that personal data obtained during the recruitment process are securely stored or are destroyed.

15.3 Pension records

There are two main regulatory sources for the retention of documents relating to occupational pension schemes:

- The Occupational Pension Schemes (Scheme Administration) Regulations 1996 (SI/1996/1715). These regulations were made to implement s 49 of the Pensions Act 1995. In the Retention Schedule the regulations are referred to as the '*Scheme Administration Regulations*' or abbreviated to the 'OPS (SA) Regs 1996'.
- The Retirement Benefits Schemes (Information Powers) Regulations 1995 (SI/1995/3103). These regulations were made under ICTA 1988. In the Retention Schedule, the regulations are either referred to as the '*Information Powers Regulations*' or abbreviated to 'RBS (IP) Regs 1995'.

i Information Powers Regulations

Regulation 15 of the Information Powers Regulations places obligations on administrators, trustees, participating employers and sponsors of Inland Revenue approved pension schemes to preserve all books, documents and other records in their possession or under their control relating to any:

- monies received or receivable by an approved scheme or a relevant statutory scheme; or
- investments or other assets held by that scheme; or
- monies paid or payable out of funds held under that scheme; or
- any annuity contract by means of which benefits provided under that scheme have been secured; or
- person who is, or has been, a controlling director of a company which is an employer in relation to the scheme.

Generally speaking, the retention period is six years from the end of the scheme year (see the Retention Schedule for the detailed requirements). The purpose of these requirements is to ensure that the documents are kept and made available for inspection by the Inland Revenue.

The duty to preserve books, documents and other records under the Retirement Benefit Schemes (Information Powers) Regulations 1995 may be discharged by the preservation of the information contained in them.

ii Scheme Administration Regulations

Under the Scheme Administration Regulations, the trustees of any trust scheme must keep records of their meetings (including meetings of any of their number) for at least six years from the end of the scheme year to which they relate (regs 12–14).

The trustees must also keep all books and records relating to any of the following transactions for at least six years from the end of the scheme year to which they relate:

- any amount received for any contribution payable for an active member of the scheme;
- the date on which a member joins the scheme;
- payments of pensions and benefits;
- payments made by or on behalf of the trustees to any person including a professional adviser and such records to include the

name and address of the person to whom payment was made and the reason for that payment;

- any movement or transfer of assets from the trustees to any person including a professional adviser and such records to include the name and address of the person to whom the assets were moved or transferred and the reason for that transaction;
- the receipt or payment of money or assets in respect of the transfer of members into or out of the scheme and such records to include, in the case of a member who has transferred into the scheme, the name of that member, the terms of the transfer, the name of the transferring scheme, the date of the transfer and date of receipt or payment of money or assets, and, in the case of a member who has transferred out of the scheme, the name of that member, the terms of the transfer, the name of the scheme transferred to, the date of the transfer, and the date of receipt or payment of money or assets;
- in a case where an appropriate policy of insurance is taken out by virtue of s 32A of the Pension Schemes Act 1993 (discharge of protected rights on winding up: insurance policies) the name of the insurance company, the name of members in respect of which the appropriate policy of insurance is taken out, the payment of money or assets and the date of such payments;
- payments made to a member who leaves the scheme, other than on a transfer, and such records to include the name of that member, the date of leaving, the member's entitlement at that date, the method used for calculating any entitlement under the scheme and how that entitlement was discharged;
- payments made to the employer; and
- other payments to, and withdrawals from, the scheme, including the name and address of the person the payment was made to or from whom it was received.

These requirements do not apply in the case of the following trust schemes (reg 12(2)):

- occupational pension schemes which provide relevant benefits but are neither approved schemes nor relevant statutory schemes;
- occupational pension schemes with less than two members;
- occupational schemes in which (i) the only benefits provided are death benefits, and (ii) under the provisions of which no member has accrued rights;

- occupational pension schemes with a superannuation fund such as is mentioned in s 615(6) of ICTA 1988.

15.4 Records of pension trustees' meetings

Regulation 13 of the Scheme Administration Regulations provides that records of the meetings of trustees of any trust scheme must be in writing and state:

- the date, time and place of the meeting;
- the names of all the trustees invited to the meeting;

Retention Schedule 5: Employment and pension records

Record Description	Regulatory retention period and source	Recommended retention period
Employment records (see 15.1)		
1 Job applications and interview records		Three months after notifying unsuccessful candidates.
2 Personnel and training records including: – Qualifications/references – Annual/assessment reports – Job history – Resignation, termination and/or retirement letters – Disciplinary matters		Six years after employment ceases.
3 Written particulars of employment, contracts of employment, and changes to terms and conditions		Six years after employment ceases.
4 Working time opt out forms	Two years after the opt-out has been rescinded or has ceased to apply: [Working Time Regulations 1998, regs 5 and 9].	

- the names of the trustees who attended the meetings and those who did not attend;
- the names of any professional advisers or any other person who attended the meeting;
- any decisions made at the meeting; and
- whether, since the previous meeting, there has been any occasion when a decision has been made by the trustees and if so, the time, place and date of such a decision and the names of the trustees who participated in the decision.

Form in which to be kept	Reasons and remarks
Original applications probably only necessary. Other records could be in any form.	Evidence to protect against actions for discrimination, etc. Data protection principles suggest short retention period unless applicants are notified otherwise.
Any.	Limitation, although health and safety and medical records may need to be kept for longer (see Retention Schedule 6).
Any.	Evidence of compliance: Written particulars must be given to employees. Employer does not need to keep paper copy.
Originals are not required by the Regulations.	Statutory.

Retention Schedule 5: Employment and pension records – *continued*

Record Description	Regulatory retention period and source	Recommended retention period
5 Records to show compliance with Working Time Regulations 1998, including: – Time sheets for opted out workers – Health assessment records for night workers	Two years: [Working Time Regulations 1998, regs 5 and 9].	
6 Annual leave records		Two years or possibly longer if leave can be carried over.
7 Welfare records		Destroy after minimum of six years after last action.
8 Senior executive records		Six years after employment ceases
9 Travel and subsistence – claims and authorisation		Six years.
10 Payroll and wage records (including details on overtime, bonuses, expenses and benefits in kind)	Unincorporated businesses – five years after 31 January next following year of assessment: [TMA 1970, ss 12 and 15]. Companies – Six years from the year end: [FA 1998, Sch 18, para 21].	

Form in which to be kept	Reasons and remarks
Any.	Statutory.
Any.	Best practice.
Any.	Best practice/Data protection.
Any.	Limitation, although some records might be kept for longer historical reasons.
Any [TMA, s 12(5)].	Tax. Tax.

Retention Schedule 5: Employment and pension records – *continued*

Record Description	Regulatory retention period and source	Recommended retention period
11 PAYE records	Not less than three years after the end of the tax year to which they relate: [Income Tax (Pay As You Earn) Regulations 2003, reg 97].	
12 Labour agreements		10 years after ceasing to be effective.
13 Works council minutes		Permanent.
14 Medical and health records		
15 Maternity pay records and certificates required to be kept by employer under by the Statutory Maternity Pay (General) Regulations 1986, reg 26	Three years after the end of the tax year in which the maternity pay period ends: [Statutory Maternity Pay (General) Regulations 1986, reg 26].	
16 Other maternity pay documentation		18 months.
17 Sickness records required for the purposes of the Statutory Sick Pay (General) Regulations 1982	Three years after the end of each tax year: [Statutory Sick Pay (General) Regulations 1982, reg 13].	
18 Complete sick absence record showing dates and causes of sick leave		Six years.

Form in which to be kept	Reasons and remarks
	See further **14.9**. Reg 97 does not apply to documents that must be sent to the Inland Revenue under the Income Tax (Pay As You Earn) Regulations 2003.
	Best Practice.
	Best Practice.
	See Retention Schedule 6.
	Certain records need to be kept even if the employer runs a contractual scheme (see Inland Revenue Booklet CA30 'Statutory Sick Pay manual for employers').
Any.	Business needs – data may need to be made anonymous for data protection purposes.

Retention Schedule 5: Employment and pension records – *continued*

Record Description	Regulatory retention period and source	Recommended retention period
19 Bank details – current		No longer than necessary.
20 Record of advances for season tickets, etc		Six years after repayment.
21 Death Benefit Nomination and Revocation Forms		While employment continues or six years after paymen of benefit.
Pension scheme records (see 15.3)		
22 All pension scheme trust deeds and rules		Life of the scheme.
23 Statement of principles and policies required by s 35 of the Pensions Act 1995		12 years after revision.
24 Pension scheme investment policies		12 years after final cessation of any benefit payable under the policy.
25 Disputes procedures		Until revised or replaced.
26 Inland revenue approvals		Life of scheme.
Occupational Pension Schemes (Scheme Administration) Regulations 1996		
27 Written appointments terms of professional advisers		Six years after appointment ceases.
28 Minutes of meetings of trustees (including meetings of any of their number)	Six years from the end of the scheme year to which they relate: OPS (SA) 1996, regs 12-14.	Life of the scheme.

Form in which to be kept	Reasons and remarks
Any.	Business needs/Data protection.
Any.	Evidence/Tax.
Any.	
Originals. Any.	If merged with another scheme, 12 years after merging. Evidence/Limitation.
Any.	Evidence/Limitation.
Any.	Required to show compliance with Pensions Act.
Originals.	Best Practice.
'In writing' [OPS(SA)].	May also be required to show compliance with Pensions Act.
'In writing' [OPS(SA), reg 13].	Best practice. See **15.4**.

Retention Schedule 5: Employment and pension records – *continued*

Record Description	Regulatory retention period and source	Recommended retention period
29 Financial records including: – any amount received for any contribution payable for an active member of the scheme; – the date on which a member joins the scheme; – payments of pensions and benefits; – payments made to professional advisers, together with the name and address of the person paid and the reason for the payment; – any movement or transfer of assets from the trustees to any person, together with the name and address of the person to whom the assets were transferred and the reason for that transaction; – payments made to a member who leaves the scheme, together with the member's name, the leaving date, the member's benefits at that date, the method used for calculating them and how they were paid; – payments made to the employer; – other payments into, and out of, the scheme including the name and address of the person the payment was made to or received from	Six years from the end of the scheme year to which they relate: [OPS (SA) 1996, regs 12 and 14].	

Form in which to be kept	Reasons and remarks
The regulations are neutral as to form.	

Retention Schedule 5: Employment and pension records – *continued*

Record Description	Regulatory retention period and source	Recommended retention period
30 Transfers into the scheme including details of the receipt of money or assets for the transfer, the member's name, the terms of the transfer, the name of the transferring scheme, the date of the transfer and date of receipt of the money or assets	Six years from the end of the scheme year to which they relate: [OPS (SA) Regs 1996, regs 12 and 14].	
31 Transfers out of the scheme including details of the payment of money or assets for the transfer, the name of the member, the terms of the transfer, the name of the scheme transferred to, the date of the transfer, and the date of payment of the money or assets	Six years from the end of the scheme year to which they relate: [OPS (SA) Regs 1996, regs 12 & 14].	
32 Details of insurance policy purchased to protect members' rights when scheme is winding up, including the name of the insurer, the names of the relevant members, the payment of money or assets and the date of such payments	Six years from the end of the scheme year to which they relate: [OPS (SA) Regs 1996, regs 12 and 14].	

Form in which to be kept	Reasons and remarks
The regulations are neutral as to form.	
The regulations are neutral as to form.	
The regulations are neutral as to form.	

Retention Schedule 5: Employment and pension records – *continued*

Record Description	Regulatory retention period and source	Recommended retention period
Retirement Benefits Schemes (Information Provision) Regulations 1995 (RBS(IP))		
33 Accounts and actuarial valuation reports relating to the scheme, including books, documents and other records on which such accounts or reports are based	Six years from the end of the scheme year in which falls the date on which the accounts were signed or, as the case may be, the report was signed: [RBS(IP), reg 15].	
34 Small self-administered schemes investment and borrowing transactions All books, documents or other records relating to: – the acquisition or disposal of land – loans by scheme to an employing company – acquisition/disposal of shares of employing company – acquisition or disposal of shares in an unlisted company – the borrowing of money – other transactions with employing company	Six years from end of scheme year in which the transaction took place: [RBS(IP), regs 5 and 15].	
35 Documents relating to events notifiable under reg 6 (employers), reg 8 (controlling directors), reg 10 (chargeable events) and reg 11 of the RBS(IP) Regulations 1995	Six years after end of scheme year in which the event to which the information relates occurred: [RBS(IP)]. reg 15	

Form in which to be kept	Reasons and remarks
Any [RBS(IP), reg 15(5)].	
Any [RBS(IP), reg 15(5)].	
Any [RBS(IP), reg 15(5)].	

Retention Schedule 5: Employment and pension records – *continued*

Record Description	Regulatory retention period and source	Recommended retention period
36 Special contribution records required by reg 7 of the RBS(IP) Regulations 1995	Six years from the end of the scheme year in which the special contribution to which the information relates was paid to the scheme: [RBS(IP), reg 15].	
37 Books, documents or other records containing information which is required to be furnished pursuant to reg 9 (payments to controlling directors)	Six years from the end of the scheme year in which the benefits to which the information relates began to be paid: [RBS(IP), reg 15].	
38 Documents relating to events specified in reg 15(4), i.e. (a) provision of any benefit to an employee, or to the widow, widower, children, dependants, or personal representatives, of an employee; (b) refund of contributions to a person who left service as an employee without entitlement to benefits under the scheme; (c) payment of contributions to the scheme by employer/ employee; (d) making of payments by the scheme to any employer;	Six years from end of scheme year in which event took place: [RBS(IP), reg 15].	

Form in which to be kept	Reasons and remarks
Any [RBS(IP), reg 15(5)].	
Any [RBS(IP), reg 15(5)].	

Retention Schedule 5: Employment and pension records – *continued*

Record Description	Regulatory retention period and source	Recommended retention period
(e) payment of transfer values or the purchase of annuities; (f) acquisition or disposal of any asset by the scheme; (g) undertaking of any transaction for the purposes of the scheme; (h) receipt of any income resulting from (i) the investment of assets held by the scheme, or (ii) any trading activity carried on by the scheme		
39 Documents re decision to allow retirement due to incapacity	Six years from end of scheme year in which benefits began: [RBS(IP), reg 15].	

Form in which to be kept	Reasons and remarks
Any [RBS(IP), reg 15(5)].	

16 Health and Safety Records

16.1 Overview

Health and safety regulations contain a number of specific requirements to retain records, some for relatively long periods. Records may be required to fulfil a statutory obligation or may be needed as a prerequisite to carrying out certain activities. Failure to hold valid documents may attract the penalties of prosecution, improvement or prohibition notices. For example, failure to maintain a register of dangerous substances under the Control of Substances Hazardous to Health (COSHH) regulations could lead to a prohibition on using such substances.

Several regulations require employers to produce and keep written assessments of health and safety risks and of the preventative measures put in place to minimise them. Such records are liable to inspection and must be kept until they are superseded or no longer relevant. Failure to produce such documentation on an inspection could result in the issue of an improvement notice.

As well as helping to avoid prosecution, health and safety records may also be useful when defending allegations of negligence in personal injury cases. Failure to provide appropriate and accurate documentation in the event of civil litigation may lead to heavy compensation payments.

16.2 Legislation

The core legislation underpinning health and safety in the United Kingdom is the Health and Safety at Work Act 1974 (HSWA). The HSWA is supplemented by a plethora of regulations, many of which have been introduced or amended to comply with European legislation. The most famous of these is a set of six regulations, known as the 'six pack', which came into operation on 1 January 1993 to implement EC Directives. Two of original regulations have subsequently been replaced, and the updated 'six pack' consists of:

- Management of Health and Safety at Work Regulations 1999 (SI/1999/3242);
- Provision and Use of Work Equipment Regulations 1998 (PUWER 1998) (SI/1998/2306);
- Workplace (Health, Safety and Welfare) Regulations 1992 (SI/1992/3004);
- Personal Protective Equipment at Work Regulations 1992 (SI/1992/2966);
- Manual Handling Operations Regulations 1992 (SI/1992/2793);
- Health and Safety (Display Screen Equipment) Regulations 1992 (SI/1992/2792).

Other important regulations include:

- Control of Substances Hazardous to Health Regulations 1999 (COSHH) (SI/1999/437);
- Reporting of Injuries, Diseases and Dangerous Occurrences Regulations 1995 (RIDDOR) (SI/1995/3163);
- Construction (Design and Management) Regulations 1994 (SI/1994/3140);
- Safety Representatives and Safety Committees Regulations 1977 (SI/1977/500);
- Health and Safety (Consultation with Employees) Regulations 1996 (SI/1996/1513);
- Electricity at Work Regulations 1989 (SI/1989/635);
- Noise at Work Regulations 1989 (SI/1989/1790);
- Health and Safety (First Aid) Regulations 1981 (SI/1981/917);
- Health and Safety (Safety Signs and Signals) Regulations 1990 (SI 1990/341);
- Health and Safety (Training for Employment) Regulations 1990 (SI/1990/1380).

Other relevant legislation includes:

- Factories Act 1961;
- Employers' Liability (Compulsory Insurance) Act 1969;
- Fire Precautions Act 1971;
- Social Security Act 1975 (the enabling legislation for the Social Security (Claims and Payments) Regulations 1979 and the Social Security (Industrial Injuries) (Prescribed Diseases) Regulations 1985).

16.3 Health and safety records

Health and safety records may fall under the following categories:

- Statutory records: e.g. accident books, fire certificates;
- Procedural records: These may be specified by regulations and will normally relate to the management of health and safety than to reporting requirements, e.g. health and safety policy statement and risk assessments, safety procedures, manuals and copies of instructions or information supplied to employees;
- Pre-employment and employment records: These could include copies of pre-employment questionnaires and medicals relating to health and safety. Employment records can contain details of health and safety training provided, information supplied and the issue of personal protective equipment;
- Medical records: These are required under a number of regulations and must usually be kept for a long period.

Apart from the existence of regulatory requirements, the primary reason for keeping health and safety records ought to be to enable the employer to protect the safety of the staff and public. Records may also useful for limiting exposure to litigation. Under the Limitation Act 1980, personal injury actions must be commenced within three years of the injury occurring. However, because many industrial injuries may not be capable of detection within that period, e.g. those relating to asbestos and noise damage, the Act allows claims to be brought within three years of the date of knowledge of the disease or injury. This considerably extends the time for which some records have to be kept. Evidence that may be needed to fight such a claim include:

- relevant risk assessments – these are formal surveys of the workplace (under the Management of Health and Safety at Work Regulations 1992) to assess any risks to health and safety to which staff and others are exposed; reviews and updates should be included;
- safe operating procedures and safe systems of work;
- effectiveness of controls such as the monitoring of noise and light levels;
- maintenance of controls and other machinery;
- medical surveillance, including pre-employment medicals and audiometry, and biological monitoring;

- training;
- safety inspections, including checks to confirm that safe operating procedures are being used and personal protective equipment is being worn;
- records of who else worked on the process and who their supervisors were;
- personal protective equipment specification, training, storage and maintenance arrangements;
- information on other employees who have suffered disease or injury as a result of the process;
- knowledge of when the disease or injury was established.

At some time it may be necessary to demonstrate that there is a history of effective safety management, for example as part of a defence against litigation or criminal prosecution, or just to show a Health and Safety Executive inspector. There may also be a case for keeping records after they have been updated or re-assessed just to provide information on long-term trends.

16.4 Form of health and safety records

Most health and safety legislation is neutral as to the form in which records must be kept. Although current procedures and policies will often need to be disseminated in paper form, many of the records associated with health and safety can be kept in computerised form. Confirmation that the form in which records are kept is suitable can be obtained, if necessary, from health and safety inspectors.

Retention Schedule 6: Health and Safety and medical records

Record Description	Regulatory retention period and source	Recommended retention period
1 Written statement of general policy with respect to the health and safety at work of employees and the organisation and arrangements for carrying out that policy	All employers must have such a written policy [HSWA, s 2(3)].	If policy is amended, previous version should be kept for a minimum of six years and possibly longer.
2 Record and minutes of consultations with safety representatives and committees		Minimum of six years.
3 General register and other records required to be kept under s 140 of the Factories Act 1961	Two years from date of last entry [Factories Act, s 141]	
4 Register of consignment notes and carriers' schedules under Special Waste Regulations 1996 (SWR)	Three years [SWR, reg 15(4)].	
5 Site records for deposit of special waste	Permanently [SWR, reg 16(1)].	
6 Consignment note for controlled waste	Two years [Environmental Protection (Duty of Care) Regulations 1991].	
7 Noise exposure assessments under reg 4(1) of the Noise at Work Regulations 1989	Until a further noise assessment is made pursuant to reg 4(1) [Reg 5].	

Form in which to be kept	Reasons and remarks
For practical reasons the current policy will need to exist in paper form. There would seem to be no reason why former policies should not be held in some other form.	Statutory/Evidence/ Evidence of compliance.
Although minute books are usually kept in paper form, there appears to be no particular reason in this case why they could not be kept in some other form.	Evidence/Evidence of compliance – Records may need to be produced on a H&S inspection but may also be of use when defending civil actions.
Paper form.	Statutory.
Likely to be in paper form.	Statutory – Records must be handed to Environment Agency if licence is surrendered or revoked.
Any.	Statutory – Records must be handed to Environment Agency if licence is surrendered or revoked.
Likely to be in paper form.	Statutory.
Any.	Records to prove that necessary preventative actions have been taken will also be needed for H&S inspections.

Retention Schedule 6: Health and Safety and medical records – *con*

Record Description	Regulatory retention period and source	Recommended retention period
8 Accident Book (Form BI 510) required by Social Security (Claims and Payments) Regulations 1979	Three years from date of each entry [Reg 25(3)].	
Reporting of Injuries, Diseases and Dangerous Occurrences Regulations 1995 (RIDDOR)		
9 Record of any reportable injury, disease and dangerous occurrence	Three years from date of entry for each reportable incident [RIDDOR, reg 7].	
Management of Health and Safety at Work Regulations 1999		
10 Significant findings of any risk assessment carried out to comply with reg 3 and any group of employees identified by it as being especially at risk	At least until a further assessment has taken place which renders the previous one obsolete [Reg 3(6)].	
Control of Substances Hazardous to Health Regulations 2002 (COSHH)		
11 Significant findings of risk assessment undertaken in accordance with reg 6	At least until a further assessment has taken place which renders the previous one obsolete [Reg 6(4)].	This type of record should b kept for a minimum of 10 years or beyond especially if ther have been potentially dangerous exposures.
12 List of employees exposed to group 3 and 4 biological agents	40 years [Reg 7 (10) and Schedule 3, para 4].	

Form in which to be kept	Reasons and remarks
Any.	Statutory – The HSE published a new version of the BI510 in 2003 that complies with data protection legislation. Accident Regulations allow paper or electronic records.
The Regulations do not specify a particular form in which records must be kept.	Statutory.
Any.	Record will be required to show compliance with regulations.
Any.	Record will be required to show compliance with regulations.
Any.	Statutory.

Retention Schedule 6: Health and Safety and medical records – *con*

Record Description	Regulatory retention period and source	Recommended retention period
13 Where exposure may lead to a disease many years later	40 years after last exposure [COSHH, Sch 9].	
14 Record of examination and maintenance of control equipment	Five years [reg 9].	
15 Record of exposure to hazardous substance at the workplace: (a) general exposure (b) personal exposure of identifiable employee	Five years [reg 10(5)(b)]. 40 years [reg 10(5)(a)].	
16 Health surveillance, including medical reports, of employees who are, or are liable to be, exposed to a substance hazardous to health	40 years from date of last entry for each individual [reg 11(3)].	
17 Record of specialist training for employees provided to comply with reg 12		At least six years after employment ceases.
18 Accident and emergency plans required by reg 13		Six years after plan has been superseded or revised, but potential value for defending civil actions should be considered.
Ionising Radiations Regulations 1999 (IRR)		
19 Record of maintenance and examination of personal protective equipment	Two years from date of examination [reg 10].	

Form in which to be kept	Reasons and remarks
Any.	Statutory.
Any.	Statutory.
Any.	Statutory.
Any.	Statutory.
Any.	Will be required for H&S inspections to show compliance with reg 12.
Any.	Current, and possibly recently replaced plans, will be required for H&S inspections to show compliance with reg 13.
Any.	Statutory.

Retention Schedule 6: Health and Safety and medical records – *cont*

Record Description	Regulatory retention period and source	Recommended retention period
20 Record of reasons for implementing a system of dose limitation	50 years [reg 11(2) and Sch 4, Pt II, para 17].	
21 Record of specialist training for employees provided to comply with reg 14		At least six years after employment ceases.
22 Radiation dosage measurements required by reg 18(3)	Two years from date measurements recorded [reg 18(5)].	
23 Record of maintenance and testing of measurement and control equipment	Two years from date records were made [reg 19(4)].	
24 Individual radiation dose assessments	Until person has attained the age of 75 but in any event for a minimum of 50 years after the records were made [reg 21(3)].	
25 Summary of radiation dose assessments	Two years from end of calendar year [reg 21(7)].	
26 Report of investigation required by reg 22	Two years after date report was made [reg 22(4)].	
27 Radiation accident assessments for individuals	Until person has attained the age of 75 but in any event for a minimum of 50 years after the records were made [reg 23(2)].	

Form in which to be kept	Reasons and remarks
Any.	Statutory.
Any.	Will be required for H&S inspections to show compliance with reg 14.
Any.	Statutory.
Any.	Statutory.
Any.	Statutory.
Any.	Statutory.
Any.	Statutory.
Any.	Statutory.

Retention Schedule 6: Health and Safety and medical records – *cont*

Record Description	Regulatory retention period and source	Recommended retention period
28 Radiation health records	Until person has attained the age of 75 but in any event for a minimum of 50 years after the records were made [reg 24(3)].	
29 Overexposure report	Until person has attained the age of 75 but in any event for a minimum of 50 years after the records were made [reg 25(2)].	
30 Record of testing of radioactive seals, etc	Two years after article is disposed of or until a further record is made following a subsequent test to that article [reg 27(3)].	
31 Records of the quantity and location of radioactive substances	Two years from the date on which they were made and, in addition, for at least two years from the date of disposal of that radioactive substance [reg 28].	
32 Reports of investigations carried out to comply with regs 30 and 32	50 years (or two years if minor incident) [regs 30(5) and 32(7)].	

Form in which to be kept	Reasons and remarks
Any.	Statutory.
Any.	Statutory.
Any.	Statutory.
Any.	Statutory.
Any.	Statutory.

Retention Schedule 6: Health and Safety and medical records – *cont*

Record Description	Regulatory retention period and source	Recommended retention period
Control of Lead at Work Regulations 2002 (CLW)		
33 Records of training to comply with reg 11		Minimum of period of employment or six years whichever is the longer.
34 Accident and emergency procedures to comply with reg 12		Should be retained for a minimum of six years after being updated.
35 Records of maintenance and examination of control measures under reg 8	Five years [reg 8(4)].	
36 Air monitoring records required under reg 9	Five years [reg 9(4)].	
37 Health surveillance of employees exposed, or liable to be exposed, to lead	40 years from date at which entry was made [reg 10(3)].	
Control of Asbestos at Work Regulations 2002 (CAWR)		
38 Significant findings of asbestos risk assessment under reg 6	Duration of the work at the premises [reg 6(4)].	
39 Plan of work required by reg 7	Duration of work at premises [reg 7(2)].	
40 Record of employee training, accident and emergency procedures		

Form in which to be kept	Reasons and remarks
Any.	Evidence/Evidence of compliance.
Current procedures will need to be in paper form for practical reasons, otherwise any.	Evidence/Evidence of compliance.
Any.	Statutory.
Any.	Statutory.
Any.	Statutory.
Any.	Statutory.
Paper probably required for practical reasons.	Statutory.
Any.	To show compliance with regs 9 and 14.

Retention Schedule 6: Health and Safety and medical records – *cont*

Record Description	Regulatory retention period and source	Recommended retention period
41 Records of maintenance and examination of control measures under reg 12	Five years [reg 12(3)].	
42 Air monitoring records when: – health surveillance required – health surveillance not required	40 years [reg 18(4)]. Five years [reg 18(4)].	
43 Health surveillance (including medical reports)	40 years from date of last entry [reg 21(1)].	
Chemical (Hazard Information and Packaging for Supply) Regulations 2002		
44 Record of information (a) used for the purposes of classifying dangerous preparations in accordance with reg 4; (b) used for the purposes of labelling in accordance with reg 8; (c) relating to any child resistant fastening or any tactile warning which forms part of the packaging in which the dangerous preparation in question is contained; and (d) used for the purposes of preparing the safety data sheet relating to that dangerous preparation in accordance with regulation 5	Three years [CHIPS, reg 12(1)].	

Form in which to be kept	Reasons and remarks
Any.	Statutory.
Any.	Statutory.
Any.	Statutory.
Any.	Statutory.

17 Contracts, sales and insurance

17.1 Contracts

The two main factors which will determine retention periods for contracts are the limitation period and the possibility that the contract is a supporting document for tax reasons. Records of contracts kept for tax reasons need not be originals. Where contracts are made on standard terms, it will normally suffice to keep a record (in any form) of the contract amounts, date, customers, etc and to keep a copy of those standard terms.

Copies of contracts and associated documents may be needed for practical and business reasons to manage the contract and its performance. Ultimately, they could be required as evidence either to defend or initiate legal actions for breach or non-performance. There is no legal requirement to retain records for these purposes. However, failure to do so could affect the outcome of such proceedings. Accordingly, decisions on the retention of contractual documentation will need to be made after a careful assessment of the risks of non-retention (see **6.2**).

As far as the limitation period is concerned, actions will no longer be possible on a simple contract six years after the cause of action accrued, e.g. non-payment. Although this will often suggest a retention period of six years after performance, if it is an ongoing contract, then it will obviously need to be retained for six years after it has been terminated or replaced. Most contracts which must be kept for tax reasons must be kept for about the same period. If a contract is executed as a deed, the limitation period is 12 years. A contract will not necessarily be a deed simply because it is executed by a company under seal. Certain actions relating to contracts and their performance may be brought after the normal limitation period has expired, e.g. where there is latent damage up to 15 years after the damage occurred. This may be particularly relevant to building contracts where retention periods will usually be longer (see **Chapter 6** and **Chapter 18**).

17.2 Marketing

Marketing departments must obtain prior consent for certain types of direct marketing and honour any request not to be sent direct marketing communications (see **7.12**). They will also need to have regard to the principles for the processing and use of personal data under the Data Protection Act 1998 for these purposes (see **Chapter 7**).

Marketing and advertising records will not often be required for regulatory or evidential reasons. Accordingly, their retention will be subject primarily to business needs.

Advertising in the UK is mainly controlled through codes of practice. In the case of advertisements in the non-broadcast media, the Advertising Standards Authority (ASA) oversees and acts to ensure compliance with the British Codes of Advertising and Sales Promotion. The Codes essentially require advertisements to be legal, decent, honest and truthful, and that they be prepared with a sense of responsibility to consumers and society at large.

However, this self-regulatory system is backed up by legislation in the form of the Control of Misleading Advertisements Regulations 1988 (as amended by the Control of Misleading Advertisements (Amendment) Regulations 2000 (SI 2000/914). These implement EU Directives on misleading and comparative advertisements. The Regulations require the Director General of Fair Trading (DGFT) to investigate complaints, and empower him to seek an injunction from the courts against publication of an advertisement, if necessary. More usually, however, he would initially seek assurances from an advertiser to modify or not repeat an offending advertisement. Before investigating, the DGFT can require that other means of dealing with a complaint, such as the ASA system mentioned above, have been fully explored. Action by the DGFT usually results only from a referral from the ASA where the self-regulatory system has not had the required impact.

Advertising in the broadcast media is subject to codes of practice formulated and enforced by the Independent Television Commission (ITC) and the Radio Authority. The Financial Services Authority (FSA) has a statutory duty to ensure that financial promotions are clear, fair and not misleading.

17.3 Sales

There is a significant body of law regulating the sales process that exists mainly for the protection and information of consumers. However, there are few, if any, direct requirements to retain records other than for accounting and tax reasons. Various records may need to be kept to prove compliance with or avoid prosecution under these laws. Relevant legislation includes the following:

i Weights and measures

Transactions in goods by weight or measure and the measuring instruments used in those transactions are in most cases regulated by the Weights and Measures Act 1985 and its secondary legislation.

ii Trade descriptions

The Trade Descriptions Act 1968 makes it an offence for a trader to apply, by any means, false or misleading statements, or to knowingly or recklessly make such statements about goods or services. The Act carries criminal penalties and is enforced by local authority Trading Standards Officers.

There are also a significant number of regulations governing the labelling of various products, e.g. in relation to food and furniture.

iii Price indications

The Price Marking Order 1999 sets out pricing requirements for products that are for sale by traders to consumers. It aims to provide price transparency for consumers. Special rules for food and drinks are provided in the Price Marking (Food and Drink Services) Order 2003 which came into force on 2 March 2004.

iv Misleading prices

The Consumer Protection Act 1987 makes it a criminal offence to mislead consumers about the price of goods, services, accommodation (including the sale of new homes) or facilities. The term 'price indication' includes price comparisons as well as indications of a single price.

17.4 Contracts for the supply of goods and services

Contracts for the supply of goods and services are subject to certain implied conditions which cannot usually be excluded. Contracts with consumers will also be subject to the Unfair Contract Terms Act 1977 and associated regulations.

i Sale of Goods Act 1979

This Act implies certain terms into contracts for the sale of goods. For example:

- goods must be as described, of satisfactory quality, and fit for any purpose which the consumer makes known to the seller;
- goods are of satisfactory quality if they reach the standard that a reasonable person would regard as satisfactory, taking into account the price and any description;
- aspects of quality include fitness for purpose, freedom from minor defects, appearance and finish, durability and safety.

The seller, not the manufacturer, is responsible under the Act. If goods are not of satisfactory quality the buyer is entitled, if he acts within a reasonable time, to reject the goods and get his money back.

The Act is now supplemented by the Sale and Supply of Goods to Consumers Regulations 2002 which came into force on 31 March 2003 and implement Directive 1999/44/EC on the Sale of Consumer Goods and Associated Guarantees.

ii Supply of Goods and Services Act 1982

This Act implies the following terms into contracts for the supply of a service:

- the service will be carried out with reasonable care and skill;
- within a reasonable time; and
- where no price has been agreed, for a reasonable charge.

These terms apply unless they have been excluded and there are strict limits on the circumstances in which an exclusion or variation will be effective. Any material used must be of satisfactory quality. The law treats the failure to meet these obligations as a breach of contract and the consumer is entitled to seek redress.

iii Unsolicited Goods and Services

Under the Unsolicited Goods and Services Act 1971 (as amended) it is an offence to demand payment for goods known to be unsolicited – if they were sent to a person without any prior request made by them or on their behalf. Someone who receives goods in these circumstances may retain them as an unconditional gift, and does not have to pay for or return, any unwanted goods.

iv Unfair Contract Terms Act 1977

Under the Unfair Contract Terms Act 1977, a person cannot exclude or restrict his liability for death or personal injury resulting from negligence. He can exclude or restrict liability for other loss or damage resulting from negligence only if the exclusion clause satisfies the test of reasonableness.

In the case of sales and hiring to consumers, a trader cannot opt out of his obligations to sell or hire goods which are of satisfactory quality. In other cases a trader dealing with a consumer or on his own written standard terms of business cannot exclude or restrict his liability for breach of contract or allow himself to provide an inadequate service unless he can show that the clause satisfies the test of reasonableness. A trader cannot require a consumer to indemnify him against any loss he may incur through negligence or breach of contract unless he can show that the clause satisfies the same test.

Whether or not a term is reasonable is for the court to decide. If a term were to be challenged, it would be for the party seeking to impose the term to demonstrate to the court that it was reasonable. The 1977 Act is drawn in this way so that commercial parties remain free to conclude contracts between themselves on such terms as they wish.

v Unfair Terms in Consumer Contract Regulations 1999

The Unfair Terms in Consumer Contracts Regulations 1999 (SI/1999/2083) provide that a term which has not been individually negotiated in a consumer contract, is unfair (and hence non-binding on the consumer) if, contrary to the requirement of good faith, it causes a significant imbalance in the rights and obligations of the parties to the detriment of the consumer.

17.5 Consumer Credit Act 1974

The Consumer Credit Act regulates consumer credit and consumer hire agreements for amounts up to £25,000. Its protections apply to agreements between traders and individuals, sole traders, partnerships and unincorporated associations, but not agreements made between traders and corporate bodies such as limited companies. The Act lays down rules covering:

- the form and content of agreements;
- credit advertising;
- the method of calculating the Annual Percentage Rate (APR) of the Total Charge for Credit;
- the procedures to be adopted in the event of default, termination, or early settlement;
- extortionate credit bargains.

The Act also requires that all traders who make regulated agreements obtain licences from the Office of Fair Trading. Credit brokers, debt advisors and others, may also require licences.

17.6 Product liability

People injured by defective products may have the right to sue for damages. In the past those injured had to prove that the manufacturer was negligent. The Consumer Protection Act 1987 removes the need to prove negligence. The Act provides the same rights to anyone injured by a defective product, whether or not the product was sold to them. A customer can also sue a supplier, without proof of negligence, under the Sale of Goods Act.

Under the Consumer Protection Act, a person can take action against:

- *Producers*: usually the manufacturer or, in the case of raw materials, the person who mined or otherwise obtained them. Also included are processors, but those involved solely in packaging are not affected unless the packaging alters the essential characteristics of the products.
- *Importers*: meaning importers into the European Community, not just into the United Kingdom. Where goods are imported into another EC country and subsequently sold in the UK, liability rests with the first importer, not the UK importer.

- *Own-branders*: suppliers who put their own name on the product and give the impression that they are the producers.
- *Other suppliers*, such as wholesalers and retailers: These are not liable unless they fail to identify the producer, importer or 'own-brander' if asked to do so by a person suffering damage.

Liability under the Act is joint and several, so the claimant may sue both (or all, if more than two) defendants. It is not possible to exclude liability under the Act by means of any contract term or other provision.

To avoid liability under the Act a commercial supplier will need to keep details of the names of producers, manufacturers or importers of goods which they sell. As this potential liability continues for ten years after the date of supply, suppliers should retain detailed records of the sources of products sold to consumers.

A number of defences are available to manufacturers and producers which, if they are to be relied upon, will require certain records to be retained. These might include instructions and safety warnings supplied with the product, the results of any quality control procedures (which may help to prove that the product was not defective at the time of supply) and records relating to product design and safety checks. Manufacturers and producers may need to retain records for these purposes for considerably longer than ten years, because the limitation provisions in Sch 1 of the Consumer Protection Act run from the date of supply to the consumer rather than the date of manufacture or production.

17.7 Insurance documents

Insurance documentation is like any other contractual documentation except that the obligations on the insurer may continue for many years. Insurance documents should generally be retained for as long as claims may be made under that policy. Insurance policies may be written either on a 'claims arising' or a 'claims made' basis. Under a 'claims arising' policy, claims may be made at any time relating to the risks insured under the policy. Under a 'claims made' policy, only claims made in the period of insurance are covered. Accordingly, 'claims arising' policies will need to be kept for much longer than 'claims made' policies. Indeed, documents relating to claims made policies may need to be kept longer for tax reasons than for commercial reasons.

Although insurance contracts, certificates, policy renewal notices, etc will need to be kept as supporting documents for tax and accounting purposes, there is no need to retain originals for these purposes. Originals will normally be kept, however, for practical reasons while it is still possible to make claims on a policy or if any claims have not yet been settled.

The underlying liabilities that are insured under insurance policies will be subject to the usual limitation periods, e.g. in relation to claims for personal injuries, etc. These limitation periods may help to place a limit on the retention of insurance contracts.

Businesses are required by law to take out certain insurance policies. It may therefore be advisable to keep certain policy certificates even though it is no longer possible to claim under that policy.

Careful records will need to be kept of incidents giving rise to claims and claims correspondence. These may be required when seeking insurance cover and for internal risk assessment purposes.

Retention Schedule 7: Contracts, sales, marketing and insurance

Record Description	Regulatory retention period and source	Recommended retention period
Contracts (see 17.1)		
1 Contracts executed as a deed		12 years after performance.
2 Other contracts		Six years after performance.
3 Contracts relating building, building maintenance, repairs, etc		15 years after performance
Sales and marketing (see 17.3–17.5)		
4 Consents for certain types of direct marketing (see **7.12**)	While still on an active marketing list.	
5 Requests to be removed from marketing lists and exception lists	Until person has been removed.	
6 Record of suppliers' details		10 years or more.
7 Standard terms and conditions		Six years.
Insurance records (see 17.7)		
8 Insurance policies renewal notices and certificates		In accordance with accounting and tax requirements or, if later, until claims under policy are barred and all outstanding claims are settled.
9 Claims correspondence		Three years after settlement

Form in which to be kept	Reasons and remarks
These are usually important enough to justify retaining the original, even if it is not required by law or practice.	Tax/Limitation.
For both tax and evidential purposes any, but originals may be preferable where contract is of significant value.	Tax/Limitation.
For both tax and evidential purposes any, but originals may be preferable where contract is of significant value.	Limitation (longer because of the possibility of latent damage).
Any.	To show compliance with regulations. Although the marketing list should itself represent a list of those who have consented, it might also need to record how that consent was given if there is more than one possibility.
Any.	Name should also be added to a permanent exception list for future reference.
	Limitation period for product liability (see **17.6**).
For both tax and evidential purposes, any.	Tax/Limitation.
For tax reasons any, but originals of policies may be preferable for the purposes of making claims.	Tax/Commercial.
Any.	Commercial.

18 Property records

18.1 Buildings records

Property records will often need to be retained for much longer than other types of records. They may be needed to prove title, rights and obligations, planning consents, compliance with building regulations, etc. Records which show wiring, plumbing, network cables and other facilities may also have great practical value.

A full record of a building's structure, plant and services is essential to plan accurately for its future maintenance and to enable occupiers to fulfil their legal obligations. Records may also contain the evidence necessary to defend unwarranted claims or to mount claims against others.

The factors which will determine retention periods for building records will include:

- evidence of title, etc – many property documents will be primary evidence of title to property and to any rights or obligations;
- limitation periods – the implications of various legislation (e.g. latent defects) will mean that certain records may have to be kept for up to 16 years (see below);
- practical value – the potential value of records for the future when maintenance, repair, alteration, refurbishment, etc of the building is proposed or planned;
- historical value – certain records of historic buildings must not be destroyed without permission.

18.2 Limitation – deeds and latent damages

The limitation period for any action on a deed is 12 years. This applies to many property transactions. It should be noted, however, that a document executed by a company under seal is not necessarily a deed, although it would be presumed to be a deed if the law requires transactions of that nature to be executed as a deed. This is important because, many property-related contracts tend to be executed under seal even though they could be executed under hand. The limitation period for these contracts will be six years unless the contract itself makes other provision.

The limitation period applicable to any claim in negligence for latent damages, other than one which includes a claim for personal injuries, is either six years from the date on which the cause of action accrues, or three years from the 'starting date', whichever is later (LA 1980, s 14A). In the latter case, there is however an overriding limitation period of fifteen years from the date on which the negligent act or omission occurred (LA 1980, s 14B). The 'starting date' is the earliest date on which the claimant first had both the right to bring the action and either actual or constructive knowledge of the damage, its cause and the person responsible (see **6.6**).

18.3 Records Centre

In view of the long-term practical value of many property records, and the evidential or intrinsic value of originals, it may be advisable to establish separate systems for their storage and retention. This could involve the creation of a special registry and archive or property records centre. Records which are likely to be of long-term value for use in the care of buildings should be identified as soon as possible and marked for transfer to the property records centre.

The following categories of records are likely to be retained in the property records centre:

- project specification;
- full sets of 'as-built' drawings;
- certificates for planning approval, compliance with building regulations, practical or substantive completion, and final completion;
- test certificates for electrical, gas, fire alarm, lift inspection, lifting equipment, hydraulic pressure, etc;
- schedules for all items of building services equipment;
- manuals for building maintenance, mechanical and electrical maintenance, manufacturers' instructions, and building users;
- copies of commissioning results of all engineering services systems;
- list of principal materials used in construction and catalogues of specialist components;
- risk assessment reports;

- list of any hazardous materials used in construction or services;
- fire precautions documents including fire consultants' reports and recommendations, statements of compliance, schedule of fire appliances, and fire certificates;
- copies of any relevant relaxation or dispensations from the Building Regulations agreed with the appropriate certifying authority;
- any defect or failure reports raised during construction or commissioning;
- copies of all guarantees on materials and workmanship;
- copies of any defects lists appended together with the names of persons responsible for remedial work;
- asset registers;
- historical narratives, for buildings on the Historic Buildings Register.

Retention and disposal schedules for buildings records should indicate records that are to be transferred to the property records centre.

Retention Schedule 8: Property records

Record Description	Regulatory retention period and source	Recommended retention period
Legal documents		
1 Deeds of title		Until sold or transferred.
2 Leases (signed copies)		15 years after expiry.
3 Subletting agreements (signed copies)		12 years after expiry or termination.
4 Wayleave agreements		12 years after expiry or termination.
5 Landlord's consents		15 years after surrender, expiry or termination of lease or memoranda of terms.

18.4 Intellectual property

Intellectual property rights may be of crucial importance to a business. Indeed the whole business may revolve around the exploitation of protected rights. Although there are very few regulatory retention requirements, records will need to be kept for practical and business reasons in relation to the registration, maintenance and protection of these rights, including records relating to:

- trade marks;
- service marks;
- registered designs;
- patents;
- copyright protection; and
- the assignment of intellectual property rights and licences granted or received in connection with them.

Form in which to be kept	Reasons and remarks
Original.	Documents of title will be transferred to new freeholder on disposal.
Original.	Documents of title. Limitation.
Original.	Limitation.
Original.	Limitation.
Original.	Limitation.

Retention Schedule 8: Property records – *continued*

Record Description	Regulatory retention period and source	Recommended retention period
6 Licences		15 years after surrender, expiry or termination of lease.
7 Planning consents		Until property sold or consent expires.
8 Listed building consents		Until property sold.
Project documents for new buildings and improvements		
9 Specifications		Up to 25 years.
10 Bills of quantity		Up to 25 years.
11 Tender documents		15 years after project completed
12 Agreements with contractors and consultants		15 years after project completed
13 Surveys and inspections		Permanently.
Reports		
14 Architectural reports		25 years.
15 Structural engineering, mechanical and electrical engineering and drainage services reports		15 years.
16 Building condition surveys		25 years.
17 Asbestos inspections		40 years +.
18 Conservation reports (Historic and listed buildings)		25 years.
19 Site surveys		25 years.
20 Maps, plans and drawings		25 years.
Maintenance records		
21 Maintenance contracts and related files		Six/12 years after end of contract.

Form in which to be kept	Reasons and remarks
Original.	Limitation.
Original.	Commercial.
Original.	Commercial.
Any.	Evidence/Limitation/Business needs.
Any.	Evidence/Limitation/Business needs.
Any.	Evidence/Limitation.
Originals preferable.	Evidence/Limitation.
Any.	Business Needs/Evidence.
Any.	Evidence/Business Needs.
Any.	Evidence/Business Needs.
Any.	Evidence/Business Needs.
Any.	Evidence/Business Needs.
Any.	Evidence/Business Needs.
Any.	Evidence/Business Needs.
	Evidence/Business Needs.
Original of contracts may be preferable, otherwise any.	Evidence/Limitation.

Retention Schedule 8: Property records – *continued*

Record Description	Regulatory retention period and source	Recommended retention period
22 Maintenance schedules and programmes		15 years.
23 Maintenance log		15 years.
Intellectual Property Records		
24 Documents evidencing assignment of trade/service marks and designs		Six years after cessation of registration.
25 Certificates of registration of trade/service marks and designs		Six years after cessation of registration.
26 Intellectual property agreements and licences		Six years after expiry.
27 Literary, dramatic and musical works for which copyright protection is claimed		Life in being + 50 years.
28 Artistic works, recordings, films, photos and broadcasts for which copyright protection is claimed		50 years.
29 Patent applications and related records		For life of patent + 50 years.
30 Applications for extension of patents		If granted, for life of patent.
31 Assignment of patent rights		For life of patent + six years.
32 Patent licences		For period of licence + six years.

Form in which to be kept	Reasons and remarks
Any.	Business needs.
Any.	
Originals preferable.	Evidence/Limitation.
Originals.	Evidence/Limitation. Copy also held in Registry.
Originals preferable.	Evidence/Limitation. Limitation period will depend on whether agreement is executed as a deed.
Any.	Evidence Copyright, Designs and Patents Act 1988.
Any.	Evidence Copyright, Designs and Patents Act 1988.
Any.	Evidence – The information will be useful for prosecuting infringements and defending patents in other ways.
Any.	Evidence – The information will be useful for prosecuting infringements and defending patents in other ways.
Assignments of patents must be 'in writing'. Accordingly, original should be kept.	Evidence/Limitation Patents Act 1977, ss 30 and 68. Assignments will usually be registered at the Patent Office.
If 'in writing', original should be kept.	Evidence/Limitation. Patent licences may be registered at the Patent Office.

Retention Schedule 8: Property records – *continued*

Record Description	Regulatory retention period and source	Recommended retention period
Records of other property assets		
33 Asset registers		Permanently.
34 MOT certificates		Until vehicle sold
35 Vehicle Registration Documents		Until vehicle sold
36 Maintenance logs		Until vehicle sold

Form in which to be kept	Reasons and remarks
Any.	Historical entries should be kept for at least six years after assets they record are sold, transferred, written off, etc.
Original.	Commercial/Best Practice.
Original.	Document of title.
Original.	Commercial/Best Practice.

19 Information management records

19.1 Introduction

This chapter deals with records that must be kept as part of the records and information management system and associated topics such as data protection and freedom of information.

19.2 Information management

Information management is concerned with the management of recorded information across the whole business, regardless of format, location or originator. Although records of information management activities need to be kept whether they relate to a paper-based, microfilm or electronic systems, the specific requirements for electronic records will tend to dictate retention policies in this area. This is not because the electronic records will necessarily be more important, but because more information will need to be retained about the policies, procedures and operation of these systems to prove the integrity of the records held on them.

Generally speaking, the requirements of the *BSI's Code of Practice for Legal Admissibility of Information Stored Electronically* (see **9.6**) should be followed together with, if applicable, the BSI Standard on the admissibility of records stored in microfilm and other microform (see **8.5**).

Information management records will include:

- policies and procedures;
- record keeping, including records management systems, retrieval, and access;
- disposal – appraisal and selection;
- storage;
- general management and administration.

19.3 Data Protection Act 1998

The requirements of the Data Protection Act 1998 must be taken into account with regard to information management policies and procedures for records containing personal data (see **Chapter 7**). Certain records may need to be kept to demonstrate compliance with the requirements of the Act, such as the organisation's policies and procedures for handling personal data.

19.4 Freedom of Information Act 2000

The Freedom of Information Act 2000 applies mainly to public bodies. Full implementation of Act must be made by 1 January 2005. For records managers the main effects of the legislation are contained in the Lord Chancellor's *Code of Practice on the Management of Records under Freedom of Information.*

The legislation and the Code impinge upon the retention of information management records in respect of disclosure decisions and the documentation of appraisal decisions. Requests for information will need to be logged so that any appeals against non-disclosure can be dealt with effectively. Those who require information have the option to seek evidence of when and why information has been disposed of. Appraisal decisions (including disposal schedules) must be recorded and this information retained permanently by the department (after 30 years this documentation needs to be covered by a retention instrument).

Retention Schedule 9: Information Management

Record Description	Regulatory retention period and source	Recommended retention period
Information management policies and procedures		
1 Information management policies		Life of business.
2 Retention and disposal schedules		Life of business.
3 Procedure manuals, guides and instructions on the management of records		Life of business.
4 Records relating to the development, implementation and review of information management policy		Five years.
5 Disaster recovery plan		Until new plan is promulgated.
6 Information surveys and record audits		Five years.
7 Information security policy		Life of business.
8 System description manuals		Life of business.
Information systems records		
9 Quality control log in relation to scanning		As long as any information kept on the system still exists.
10 System maintenance log		As long as any information kept on the system still exists.

Form in which to be kept	Reasons and remarks
Any.	To comply with BSI Code of Practice DISC PD 0008: 1999 (see **9.6**).
Any.	To comply with BSI Code of Practice DISC PD 0008: 1999 (see **9.6**).
Any.	To comply with BSI Code of Practice DISC PD 0008: 1999 (see **9.6**).
Any.	Will be helpful when reviewing policies and procedures.
Any.	
Any.	
Any.	To comply with BSI Code of Practice DISC PD 0008: 1999 (see **9.6**).
Any.	To comply with BSI Code of Practice DISC PD 0008: 1999 (see **9.6**).
Any.	To comply with para 6 of Annex C of the BSI Code of Practice DISC PD 0008: 1999 (see **9.6**).
Any.	To comply with para 4.12 of the BSI Code of Practice DISC PD 0008: 1999 (see **9.6**).

Retention Schedule 9: Information Management – *continued*

Record Description	Regulatory retention period and source	Recommended retention period
11 Audit trail data on: – information capture – batch information – indexing – change control – destruction of information – workflow		Audit trail data should be stored for at least as long as the information to which it refers. Data regarding destruction should be kept for longer
12 Certificates of compliance with BSI Code of Practice DISC PD 0008: 1999		As long as any information kept on the system at the time of certification still exists.
Records/information management records		
13 Review lists		Five years.
14 Lists, certificates, docket books or databases of records destroyed		Life.
15 Schedules of records loaned to other organisations		Until disposal of the records covered.
16 Register of records held which belong to other organisations		As long as record is held.
Storage		
17 Copies of catalogues/lists of records transferred to storage		Five years.
18 Retrieval of records from storage		Two years.
19 Security of records		Five years.
20 Records of tracking and location systems		When system is superseded.
21 Records relating to the use of on-site storage areas		Two years.

Form in which to be kept	Reasons and remarks
Any.	To comply with Chapter 6 of the BSI Code of Practice DISC PD 0008: 1999 (see **9.6**).
Any.	To comply with para 6.2.4 of the BSI Code of Practice DISC PD 0008: 1999 (see **9.6**).
Any.	
Any.	
Any.	
Any.	
Any.	
Any.	
Any.	
Any.	

Retention Schedule 9: Information Management – *continued*

Record Description	Regulatory retention period and source	Recommended retention period
22 Records relating to the transfer of records to on-site storage		Two years after records disposed
23 Records relating to the selection of off-site storage facilities		Two years.
24 Records relating to contracts with storage providers		Six years from end of contract.
25 Records relating to the transfer or retrieval of records to or from off-site storage		Two years after records disposed of.
General		
26 General administrative records and correspondence		Two years.
27 Training records, including audio visual material		Five years or until superseded.
Data Protection Act 1998 (see Chapter 7)		
28 Consents for the processing of personal and sensitive data	For as long as the data is processed and held in respect of a living individual [First Data Protection Principle].	
29 Requests for information from data subjects		
Freedom of Information Act (see 19.4)		
30 Documentation relating to the disclosure status of records under FOI		Five years after the record is opened.
31 FOI requests: a) for documents already open b) for documents which are subsequently opened c) for documents which remain closed.		One year. Two years. 10 years

Form in which to be kept	Reasons and remarks
Any.	
Any.	
Any.	
Any.	
Any.	
Any.	
Any.	Exemptions may apply for personal data but consent will nearly always be required for sensitive data.
Any.	
Any.	PRO Guidance. The FOI Act applies to public sector bodies only.
Any.	PRO Guidance. The FOI Act applies to public sector bodies only.

20 Financial services and money laundering

20.1 Introduction

This chapter deals with retention requirements imposed by:
- money laundering regulations which may be relevant to businesses that are outside, as well as within, the financial services sector; and
- the Financial Services Authority (FSA) on regulated firms in the financial services sector.

20.2 Money Laundering

Under the Money Laundering Regulations 2003, a relevant business (see definition below) must:
- adopt procedures to identify clients;
- keep records of how their identity was established and of transactions with clients;
- establish procedures to ensure the reporting of suspected money laundering activities;
- establish procedures to forestall and prevent money laundering; and
- ensure that relevant employees are aware of the money laundering regulations and given training on how to recognise and deal with transactions which may be related to money laundering.

i Record-keeping requirements

Under the Regulations, a relevant business must keep the following records:
- where evidence of identity is obtained under the identification procedures stipulated by the regulations –
  - a copy of that evidence,
  - information as to where a copy of that evidence may be obtained, or

- – information enabling the evidence of identity to be re-obtained, but only where it is not reasonably practicable for A to comply with points 1 or 2; and
- a record containing details relating to all transactions carried out in the course of relevant business.

For records mentioned in point 1 above, the retention period is:

- at least five years commencing with the date on which any business relationship ends; or
- in the case of a one-off transaction (or a series of such transactions), at least five years commencing with the date of the completion of all activities taking place in the course of that transaction (or, as the case may be, the last of the transactions).

For the records mentioned in point 2 above, the retention period is at least five years commencing with the date on which all activities taking place in the course of the transaction in question were completed.

The FSA also imposes specific retention requirements on regulated firms regarding money laundering (see Entries 61–65 in Retention Schedule 10 below). These are very similar to the regulatory requirements described above, but also require a record of any disclosures and information not acted upon to be kept. All businesses subject to the Money Laundering Regulations should follow these recommendations even though they may not be subject to FSA regulation.

ii Relevant business

For the purposes of the Regulations, a 'relevant business' includes:

- firms authorised under the Financial Services and Markets Act 2000 to carry out a regulated activity;
- bureau de change, cheque cashing and money transmission services;
- banks;
- estate agents;
- casino operators;
- insolvency practitioners;
- tax advisers;
- accountancy services;
- auditors;
- anyone providing legal services relating to a financial or real property transaction;

- any business which provides services in relation to the formation, operation or management of a company or a trust; or
- any business that deals in goods of any description (including auctioneers) whenever a transaction involves accepting a total cash payment of €15,000 or more.

20.3 FSA Handbook requirements

The FSA imposes a huge number of retention requirements on regulated firms. Retention Schedule 10 summarises the general requirements of the FSA Handbook but does not cover the:

- specific requirements for banks, building societies, friendly societies, insurers or investment businesses (these are currently

Retention Schedule 10: Financial Services

Record description	Retention period
Senior Management Arrangements, Systems and Controls (SYSC)	
1 Arrangements made to satisfy SYSC 2.1.1R (apportionment) and SYSC 2.1.3R (allocation)	Six years from the date on which the record is superseded by a more up-to-date record.
2 Matters and dealings (including accounting records) which are the subject of requirements and standards under the regulatory system	Adequate.
Conduct of Business (COB)	
3 Periodic reports on details of soft commission agreements	Three years (from termination of relevant soft commission agreement).
4 Disclosable commission – each payment	Six years.
5 Indirect benefits given to an independent intermediary each benefit	Six years.

contained in the relevant interim prudential pourcebook); or

- requirements of the Listing Rules (these are dealt with elsewhere in this Guide, although there are very few relevant requirements).

Although the FSA imposes fairly onerous retention requirements on regulated firms, its general approach to document retention and, in particular, the clarity of its Handbook in this regard, makes it a model regulator for these purposes. Each section of the FSA Handbook includes an a summary of the retention requirements imposed by that section – a model that others would do well to adopt.

The FSA's requirements can, for the most part, be satisfied by keeping records in almost any form. This can even include recordings of telephone conversations, which is often the preferred method of keeping information regarding transactions made by dealers and brokers.

FSA Handbook reference	When record must be made
SYSC 2.2.1R.	On making the arrangements and when they are updated.
SYSC 3.2.20R.	Adequate time.
COB 2.2.20R(1).	Date of periodic statement.
COB 2.2.20R(2).	Date of payment.
COB 2.2.20R(3).	Date from which benefit was conferred.

Retention Schedule 10: Financial Services – *continued*

Record description	Retention period
6 Name of individual who confirmed compliance or approved of non-real time financial promotion – Pension transfer, Pension opt-out and FSAVC – Life policy, Pension contract, or Stakeholder pension scheme – any other case	 Indefinitely. Six years (from date of confirmation or approval). Three years (from date of confirmation or approval).
7 Classification of each client – if relevant to: – Pension transfers, Pension opt-outs and FSAVCs – Life policies, Pension contracts – any other case	 Indefinitely. Six years (from end of client relationship) Three years (from end of client relationship)
8 Terms of business for: – Pension transfer, Pension opt-out or FSAVC – Life policy, Pension contract or Stakeholder pension scheme – any other case	 Indefinitely. Six years (from the date on which the customer ceases to be a customer). Three years (from the date on which the customer ceases to be a customer).
9 Adoption of a packaged product – decision to adopt	Throughout the period the adoption remains in effect and for six years thereafter
10 Private customer's details, including personal financial circumstances, for – a pension transfer, pension opt-out, FSAVC – a life policy, pension contract or stakeholder pension scheme – any other case	 Indefinitely. Six years. Three years.

FSA Handbook reference	When record must be made
COB 3.7.1R.	
COB 4.1.16R.	
COB 4.2.14R.	
COB 5.1.4R(3).	
COB 5.2.9R.	

Retention Schedule 10: Financial Services – *continued*

Record description	Retention period
11 Private customer: Opt out or transfer from an OPS on an execution only basis or Execution only transaction, no investment advice given	Indefinitely.
12 Private customer suitability letter relating to: – a pension opt-out or transfer, or FSAVC – a life policy, pension contract, or stakeholder pension scheme – any other case	Indefinitely. Six years. Three years.
13 Firm's advice to private customer who instructs a pension opt-out or transfer contrary to advice of firm and instructions to firm to proceed	Indefinitely.
14 Statistics of pension opt-out or pension transfer transactions – Details of the notification required by COB 5.3.26R(1) and (1A)	Indefinitely.
15 Statistics of pension opt-out, pension transfer or FSAVC transactions involving private customers	Indefinitely.
16 Direct offer personal pension scheme – record of justification for promotion	Six years.
17 Non-tradable life policy: Sufficient information to support classification that own policies are not tradable	Indefinitely.

FSA Handbook reference	When record must be made
COB 5.2.10R.	
COB 5.3.19AR.	
COB 5.3.25R.	
COB 5.3.26R(2).	On making the notification.
COB 5.3.27R.	On arranging the transaction.
COB 5.3.28R.	On making the promotion.
COB 6.5.52R.	Upon assessment of the firm's position and every six months thereafter.

Retention Schedule 10: Financial Services – *continued*

Record description	Retention period
18 Projections provided to a customer relating to:	
– a pension transfer or pension opt-out	Indefinitely.
– a life policy, pension contract or stakeholder pension scheme	Six years.
– any other case	Three years.
19 Cancellation or withdrawal (to include a copy of any receipt of notice issued to the customer and the customer's original notice instructions) relating to:	
– Pension transfer, opt-out or FSAVC	Indefinitely.
– Life policy, pension contract or stakeholder pension scheme	Six years (from the date when the firm became aware that notice of cancellation had been served).
– any other case	Three years (from the date when the firm became aware that notice of cancellation had been served).
20 Firm effecting or carrying out pure protection contracts – adequate details of information provided	Six years.
21 Firm effecting or carrying out general insurance contracts – adequate details of information provided	Three years.
22 Allocation of aggregated transactions in a series of transactions all executed within one business day – the time each transaction is made	

FSA Handbook reference	When record must be made
COB 6.6.19R.	As soon as proposal proceeds.
COB 6.7.47R.	Upon notice of cancellation or withdrawal being served to firm, its appointed representative or agent.
COB 6.8.18R(1).	After information provided.
COB 6.8.18R(2).	After information provided.
COB 7.7.6E(4).	On executing an aggregated transaction.

Retention Schedule 10: Financial Services – *continued*

Record description	Retention period
23 An aggregated transaction that includes a customer order – identity of each customer; whether transaction is in whole or in part for discretionary managed investment portfolio and any relevant proportions	Three years.
24 Firm aggregating a number of client orders that include a customer order – intended basis of allocation	Three years.
25 Aggregation of one or more customer orders and an own account order – intended basis of allocation	Three years.
26 Allocation of an aggregated transaction that includes the execution of a customer order – Date + time of allocation; relevant designated investment; identity of each customer and market counterparty and the amount allocated to each customer and market counterparty; agreement to extend allocation period for intermediate customers under COB 7.7.6E(2)(b)	Three years.
27 Re-allocation – Basis and reason for any re-allocation.	Three years.
28 Lending to private customers – Assessment of a private customer's financial standing and the date when the information was last updated/ checked	Three years (from the date on which the credit arrangement ceased).

FSA Handbook reference	When record must be made
COB 7.7.14R(1).	On executing an aggregated transaction.
COB 7.7.14R(2).	As soon as is practicable.
COB 7.7.14R(3).	Before the transaction is executed.
COB 7.7.16R.	Date on which the order is allocated.
COB 7.7.17R.	At the time of the re-allocation.
COB 7.9.7R.	Upon assessment.

Retention Schedule 10: Financial Services – *continued*

Record description	Retention period
29 Customer orders – Customer's name (or designation)/ account number; date and time of receipt or decision by the firm to deal; who received the order or made the decision to deal; the designated investment; the number of/total value of the designated investment including any price limit; whether sale or purchase; any other instructions received	Three years (after the date of completion of the transaction).
30 Execution of a transaction by a firm – Name/other designation of client (if any); name of counterparty (if known); date and time of execution; who executed the transaction; the designated investment; number of/ total value of the designated investment; price and other significant terms; whether sale or purchase	Three years (after the date of completion of the transaction).
31 The firm instructs another person to deal – Name of the person instructed; terms of instruction and date and time of instruction	Three years (after the date of completion of the transaction).
32 Personal account dealing – The restrictions upon pa dealing and the basis upon which any permission to deal is made	Three years (from the date that the restrictions or basis were communicated to the employee).
33 Personal account dealing – Each permission to deal given by the firm	Three years (from the date that the permission was given).

FSA Handbook reference	When record must be made
COB 7.12 3R and COB 7.12.6E(1).	When the order arises.
COB 7.12.3R and COB 7.12.6E(2).	When the firm executes a transaction.
COB 7.12.3R and COB 7.12.6E(3).	When the firm instructs another person to deal.
COB 7.13.11R(1)(a).	Whenever the restrictions are placed and from the date of consent.
COB 7.13.11R(1)(b).	From the date of consent.

Retention Schedule 10: Financial Services – *continued*

Record description	Retention period
34 Personal account dealing – Each notification of the transaction made by the employee to the firm	Three years (from the date that the notification was made).
35 Personal account dealing – The basis upon which the firm has determined that an employee will not be involved in, or have access to information about, the firm's designated investment business	Three years (from the date on which the individual ceases to be an employee).
36 Confirmation of transaction – Information provided	Three years.
37 Periodic statements	Three years.
38 Allocation of aggregated transactions in a series of transactions all executed within one business day – The time each transaction is made	
39 Aggregated transaction on behalf of a number of schemes – Identity of schemes concerned, whether transaction was effected proportionally or if a stated proportion was effected for some schemes under its management	
40 Aggregated customer orders on behalf of a number of schemes – The intended basis of allocation	
41 Aggregated orders of schemes under its management and own account orders – The intended basis of allocation	
42 Periodic statements in relation to unregulated collective investment scheme	Three years.

FSA Handbook reference	When record must be made
COB 7.13.11R(1)(c).	From the date of notification.
COB 7.13.11R(1)(d).	On determining the basis.
COB 8.1.14R.	On dispatch of confirmation.
COB 8.2.9R.	On date on which it is provided.
COB 10.3.3E(3).	On executing an aggregated transaction.
COB 10.3.5R(1).	On executing an aggregated transaction.
COB 10.3.5R(2).	As soon as is practicable.
COB 10.3.5R(3).	Before the transaction is executed.
COB 10.7.6R.	On providing the periodic statement.

Retention Schedule 10: Financial Services – *continued*

Record description	Retention period
43 PTP appointment – Details of the written delegation to a PTP, PTP's undertaking under COB11.6.1R(3) and of any variation in the documentation	Three years (from date of end of the PTP's appointment).
44 Trustee firm following (or rejecting) proper advice in relation to exercise of power of investment – Evidence of compliance with COB 11.8.5R	Three years.
Client Assets (CASS)	
45 A personal investment firm that temporarily holds a client's designated investments – Client details and any actions taken by the firm	Three years (from the making of the record).
46 Safe custody: arrangements for clients ordinarily outside the United Kingdom – the steps taken and result under CASS 2.3.6R(1)(c)	Three years.
47 Client custody assets held or received by or on behalf of a client or which the firm has arranged for another to hold or receive (Full details)	Three years.
48 Safe custody investments used for stock lending activities – The identity of safe custody investments available to be lent, and those which have been lent	Three years.
49 Client money – Sufficient records to show and explain firm's transactions and commitments	Three years (after records made).

FSA Handbook reference	When record must be made
COB 11.7.1R.	On the PTP's appointment.
COB 11.8.7R.	Date on which proper advice is received.
CASS 2.1.9R.	
CASS 2.3.6R(1)(c.)	On determination that client does not wish to execute agreement.
CASS 2.6.15R.	On receipt.
CASS 2.6.16R.	On receipt.
CASS 4.3.111R.	Maintain current full details.

Retention Schedule 10: Financial Services – *continued*

Record description	Retention period
50 Client money shortfall – Each client's entitlement to client money shortfall at the failed bank	Until client repaid.
51 Client money shortfall – Each client's entitlement to client money shortfall at the failed intermediate broker, settlement agent or OTC counterparty	Until client repaid.
52 Client money shortfall – Each client's entitlement to client money shortfall at the failed intermediate broker, settlement agent or OTC counterparty	Until client repaid.
53 Adequate records and internal controls in respect of the firm's use of mandates (see CASS 4.5.5R(1) to (4)) – Up-to-date list of firm's authorities, all transactions entered into, important client documents held by the firm	
Market Conduct (MAR)	
54 Price stabilising action Full details as noted in MAR 2.7.2R	Three years.
55 Non-Market Price Transactions Details of steps taken in consideration of NMPTs	Three years.
Training and Competence (TC)	
56 Data on competence	Employment plus three years? For PTS indefinite.
57 Approved examinations – examination time limits	Employment plus three years or for PTS indefinite.

FSA Handbook reference	When record must be made
CASS 4.4.24R(3).	Maintain up-to-date records.
CASS 4.4.25R(3).	Maintain up-to-date records.
CASS 4.4.31R(3).	Maintain up-to-date records.
CASS 4.5.5R.	Maintain current full details.
MAR 2.7R.	On initiation of stabilising action.
MAR 3.5.4.	On considering the transaction.
TC 2.4.9 G.	On a continuing basis.
TC 2.5.1 R.	When employee begins in the activity.

Retention Schedule 10: Financial Services – *continued*

Record description	Retention period
58 Approved examinations – examination passes and dates and other relevant data such as periods of absence	Employment plus three years or for PTS indefinite.
59 Approved examinations – regulatory module only – criteria for application of TC 2.5.5 R to the employee	Employment plus three years or for PTS indefinite.
60 Maintaining Competence – Criteria for and application of assessment	Employment plus three years or for PTS indefinite.
61 Supervising and monitoring – Criteria in deciding level of supervision and how it is carried out	Employment plus three years or for PTS indefinite.
62 Compliance with sourcebook – Data on competence, relevant to compliance with the sourcebook.	Employment plus three years or for PTS indefinite.
Money Laundering (ML)	
63 Customer identification – Full details of evidence of identity	Five years from end of relationship with client.
64 Transactions – Full details	Five years from the date when the transaction was completed.
65 Insolvent client – Grounds for insolvency and details of steps taken to recover the debt	Five years from date of insolvency.
66 Internal and external reporting – Full details of actions taken	Five years from the creation of the record.
67 Information not acted upon – Full details of information considered by the MLRO but not made an external report	Five years from the obtaining of the information.

FSA Handbook reference	When record must be made
TC 2.5.2 G	Duration of time limits for that activity.
TC 2.5.6 G.	At the time of the application of the rule.
TC 2.6.4 G.	On a continuing basis after competence.
TC 2.7.6 G.	When the employee begins in the activity and on an ongoing basis.
TC 2.8.1 R (1).	When the employee begins in the activity and on a continuing basis.
ML 7.3.2 R (1)(a).	As soon as reasonably practicable after first contact.
ML 7.3.2 R (1)(b).	On effecting the transaction.
ML 7.3.2 R (1)(c).	When firm becomes aware of event and takes steps.
ML 7.3.2 R (1)(d).	Once actions have been taken.
ML 7.3.2 R (1)(e).	Once decision not to report has been made.

Retention Schedule 10: Financial Services – *continued*

Record description	Retention period
Supervision (SUP)	

68   Appointed representatives
   (1) Representative's name
   (2) Copy of the original contract with the appointed representative and any subsequent amendments to it (including details of any restrictions placed on the activities which the appointed representative may carry on)
   (3) Date and reason for terminating or amending the contract
	Three years from termination or amendment of the contract.

69 UK firm exercising EEA right (a) the services or activities it carries on from a branch in, or provide cross-border services into, another EEA State under that EEA right; and the requisite details or relevant details relating to those services or activities (if applicable)	Three years from the earlier of the date on which: (a) it was superseded by a more up-to-date record; or (b) the UK firm ceased to have a branch in, or carry cross-border services into, any EEA State under an EEA right.

70   Exercise of passport rights by UK firms
   (1) Services or activities carried on from a branch in, or cross-border into, another EEA State under an EEA right
   (2) The requisite details or relevant details (if applicable)
	Three years from earlier of:
	(1) record being superseded;
	(2) firm ceasing to have any EEA branches or cross-border services.

FSA Handbook reference	When record must be made
SUP 12.9.1R, SUP 12.9.2R.	On appointment, amendment of contract or termination of contract.
SUP 13.11.	Not specified.
SUP 13.11.1R.	Not specified.

Retention Schedule 10: Financial Services – *continued*

Record description	Retention period
71 Persistency reports and data reports – Records to enable the firm to monitor regularly the persistency of life policies and stakeholder pensions effected through each of its representatives and make the required reports to the FSA.	Not specified.
Dispute Resolution (DISP)	
72 Complaints subject to DISP 1.4-DISP 1.6.	Three years.
Collective Investment Schemes	
73 Instruments of Transfer – Full Details	Six years.
74 General record- keeping obligations (ACD) such as to demonstrate compliance with the rules in CIS	As implicit from the rules in CIS.
75 Dilution record- keeping obligations (ACD) – How the ACD calculates and estimates dilution and its policy and method for determining the amount of any dilution levy or dilution adjustment.	Six years.
76 General record-keeping obligations (manager) such as to demonstrate compliance with the rules in CIS	As implicit from the rules in CIS. Six years for units.
77 Dilution record-keeping obligations (manager) – How the manager calculates and estimates dilution and its policy and method for determining the amount of any dilution levy or dilution adjustment.	Six years.

FSA Handbook reference	When record must be made
SUP 16.8.23R.	Not specified.
DISP 1.5.1R.	On receipt.
CIS 6.3.1R.	From registration.
CIS 7.3.3R(1) and (2).	As implicit from the rules in CIS.
CIS 7.3.3R(3).	As implicit from the rules in CIS.
CIS 7.8.3R(1), (2) and (3).	As implicit from the rules in CIS.
CIS 7.8.3R(4).	As implicit from the rules in CIS.

Appendix A: Arthur Andersen trial – sequence of events

According to evidence submitted during the trial, the sequence of events leading to the trial of Arthur Andersen for obstructing the investigation of accounting irregularities at Enron was as follows:

9 October 2001:   Correctly anticipating litigation and government investigations, Andersen retained an experienced New York law firm to handle future Enron-related litigation.

10 October 2001:   Andersen executives discuss the advantages of shredding documents that might be of use to those suing Andersen. 'If it's destroyed through the course of normal policy and litigation is filed the next day, that's great,' Michael Odom, a senior partner in the Houston office, said during the videotaped conference among Andersen offices. 'Whatever there was that might have been of interest to somebody is gone and is irretrievable.' Odom referred to recent litigation and how extraneous memos increase the cost of document retrieval for lawsuits and could require extra explanation. 'It's embarrassing, and it's extra work for us to have those hang around,' Odom said. 'All that needs to be explained should be included in the firm's audit work papers, the final documents that must be retained for legal reasons', he said.

12 October 2001:   Five days before the SEC opened an informal inquiry into Enron, Andersen lawyer Nancy Temple sent a company e-mail reminding workers of the firm's retention and disposal policy. The policy calls for the retention of papers, e-mails and other materials considered important to projects and to destroy drafts, extraneous or redundant documents or other items considered unnecessary. Temple's e-mail to David Duncan, Andersen's lead audit partner on the Enron account, said it 'might be useful' to remind the Enron audit team of the firm's documentation and retention policy. 'It will be helpful to make sure that we have complied with the policy.'

16 October 2001:   Enron issues a press release announcing a $618 million net loss for the third quarter of 2001. That same day, but not as part of the press release, Enron announced to analysts that it would reduce shareholder equity by approximately $1.2 billion. The market reacted immediately and the stock price of Enron shares plummeted.

17 October 2001:   The SEC opened its inquiry into Enron, requesting information in writing from Enron.

19 October 2001:   Enron alerted the Andersen audit team that the SEC had begun an inquiry regarding the Enron 'special purpose entities' and the involvement of Enron's Chief Financial Officer. The next morning, an emergency conference call among high-level Andersen management was convened to address the SEC inquiry. During the call, it was decided that documentation that could assist Enron in responding to the SEC was to be assembled by the Andersen auditors.

23 October 2001:   After spending Monday 22 October 2001 at Enron, Andersen partners assigned to the Enron engagement team launched a wholesale destruction of documents at Andersen's offices in Houston, Texas. Andersen personnel were called to urgent and mandatory meetings. Instead of being advised to preserve documentation so as to assist Enron and the SEC, Andersen employees on the Enron engagement team were instructed by Andersen partners and others to destroy immediately documentation relating to Enron, and told to work overtime if necessary to accomplish the destruction. During the next few weeks, tons of paper relating to the Enron audit were promptly shredded as part of the orchestrated document destruction. The shredder at the Andersen office at the Enron building was used virtually constantly and, to handle the overload, dozens of large trunks filled with Enron documents were sent to Andersen's main Houston office to be shredded. A systematic effort was also undertaken and carried out to purge the computer hard-drives and e-mail system of Enron-related files. In addition, instructions were given to Andersen personnel working on Enron audit matters in Portland, Chicago and London to make sure that Enron documents were destroyed there as well.

8 November 2001:   The SEC served Andersen with the anticipated subpoena relating to its work for Enron. In response, members of the Andersen team on the Enron audit were alerted finally that there could be 'no more shredding' because the firm had been 'officially served' for documents.

Appendix B: Sources of Information

Organisations

Association for Information and Image Management (AIIM)

The IT Centre
8 Canalside
Lowesmoor Wharf
Worcester WR1 2RR

Tel: 01905 727600
Fax: 01905 727609
Email: info@aiim.org.uk
Web: www.aiim.org.uk/

The AIIM is a global trade association for both users and providers of enterprise content management systems for:

- Information capture
- Document management
- Workflow and BPM
- Records management
- Portals and web services
- Content management
- Data storage and archiving
- Knowledge management

AIIM activities include industry representation, user education, industry events, market research and standards making. It also publishes a free magazine 'mID' – Managing Information and Documents.

British Standards Institute (BSI)

Head Office
389 Chiswick High Road,
London W4 4AL
Tel: 020 8996 9000

For ordering standards
Tel: 01442 230442
Email: Info@bsi-global.com
Web: www.bsi.org.uk/

The BSI publishes several standards and codes that are relevant to retention issues. A detailed list of relevant publications is included in this Appendix. Publications can be ordered from its website or by telephone. It is also possible to subscribe for a service which enables on-line viewing.

Institute of Chartered Secretaries and Administrators (ICSA)

16 Park Crescent, London W1B 1AH
Tel: 020 7580 4741
Web: www.icsa.org.uk/

Updates on regulatory retention requirements may be occasionally be posted on the ICSA website (or the ICSA Publishing website).

Public Records Office (PRO)

Kew, Richmond, Surrey TW9 4DU.

Tel: 020 8876 3444
Fax: 020 8392 5286,
Web: www.pro.gov.uk/

The Public Records Office website includes useful guidance on a range of retention issues. Although these publications are targeted at government and public bodies, they will also be of broader interest, particularly in relation to issues such as electronic records, and website and e-mail retention.

Records Management Society of Great Britain

Woodside
Coleheath Bottom
Speen
Princes Risborough
Buckinghamshire
HP27 0SZ

Tel: 01494 488599
Fax: 01494 488590
e-mail: rms@rms-gb.org.uk
Web: www.rms-gb.org.uk/

The Records Management Society of Great Britain was launched in 1983. Anyone concerned with records and information, regardless of their professional or organisational status or qualifications, can join the Society. Organisations wishing to develop records or information systems and those which provide services in these fields are also welcome.

The Society's website includes a useful list of records management consultants.

The Society holds regular meetings to hear guest speakers or to hold discussions on topics as wide-ranging as office technology, organisation of records services, legal aspects of records management and the role of service companies. It is also developing its own training programmes and has a range of technical publications and information.

Society of Archivists

Prioryfield House, 20 Canon Street, Taunton, Somerset, TA1 1SW

Tel: 01823 327030
Fax: 01823 371719
Email: offman@archives.org.uk
Web: www.archives.org.uk/

The Society of Archivists is a professional body for archivists, archive conservators and records managers in the United Kingdom and Ireland. Organisations can join as affiliated members The Society's website has a number of useful publications.

BSI Publications

The most important BSI publications are highlighted in bold type in the following list.

Document management

BS 1467:1972	Specification for folders and files
BS 5097-1:1974	Specification for loose-leaf binders. Ring binders with metal mechanisms
BS 5261-1:2000	Copy preparation and proof correction. Design and layout of documents
BS 6529:1984	Recommendations for examining documents, determining their subjects and selecting indexing terms
PD ISO/TR 15489-2:2001	Records management. Guidelines
PD ISO/TR 20983:2003	Performance indicators for electronic library services
BS ISO 690-2:1997	Bibliographic references. Electronic documents or parts thereof
BS ISO 15489-1:2001	Records management. General
BS ISO 832:1994	Bibliographic description and references. Rules for the abbreviation of bibliographic terms
BS ISO 999:1996	Guidelines for the content, organization and presentation of indexes
BS EN ISO 9706:2000	Paper for documents. Requirements for permanence
BS ISO 11108:1996	Archival paper. Requirements for permanence and durability
BS ISO 11798:1999	Permanence and durability of writing, printing and copying on paper. Requirements and test methods
BS ISO 15836:2003	The Dublin Core metadata element set
BS EN 82045-1:2001, IEC 82045-1:2001	Document management. Principles and methods
03/310366 DC, IEC 82045-2	Document management. Part 2. Metadata elements and information reference model

Electronic

BS 7083: 1996	Guide to the accommodation and operating environment for information technology
BS 7799: 2002	**Code of practice for information security management**
BD 7799-1:2000	Information technology. Code of practice for information security management
BS 7799-2:2002	Information security management. Specification with guidance for use
BIP 0008: 2004	**Legal admissibility and evidential weight of information stored electronically**
BIP 0009: 2004	**Compliance workbook for use with BIP 0008**
DISC PD 0010: 1997	**Principles of good practice for information management**
DISC PD 0016: 2001	**Document scanning. Guide to scanning business documents**
DISC PD 0023: 2001	Test target for assessing output quality of black-and-white document scanners in accordance with BS ISO 12653
DISC PD 3000	Information security management. An introduction
DISC PD 3001	Preparing for BS 7799 certification
DISC PD 3002	Guide to BS 7799 risk assessment and risk management
DISC PD 3003	Are you ready for a BS 7799 audit?
DISC PD 3004	Guide to BS 7799 auditing

Microfilm

BS 1153:1992	Recommendations for processing and storage of silver-gelatine-type microfilm
BS 5444:1977	Recommendations for preparation of copy for microcopying
BS 5525:1977	Specification for 35 mm microcopying of maps and plans
BS 5536:1988	Recommendations for preparation of technical drawings for microfilming

BS 5699-1:1979, ISO 4331-1977	Processed photographic film for archival records. Specifications for silver-gelatin type on cellulose ester base
BS 5699-2:1979, ISO 4332-1977	Processed photographic film for archival records. Specifications for silver-gelatin type on poly(ethylene terephthalate) base
BS 6313:2003	Micrographics. 35 mm microfilming of serials. Specification
BS 6359:1983	Specification for dimensions and position of micro-fiche heading coating (colour stripe)
BS 6498:2002	**Guide to preparation of microfilm and other micro-forms that may be required as evidence**
BS 6660:1985	Guide to setting up and maintaining micrographics units
BS 7555:1992	Guide to miniaturization of medical diagnostic images on film
PD ISO/TR 12036:2000	Micrographics. Expungement, deletion, correction or amendment of records on microforms
BS ISO 1116:1999	Micrographics. 16 mm and 35 mm microfilm spools and reels. Specifications
BS ISO 3272	Microfilming of technical drawings and other drawing office documents.
Part 1: 2003	Operating procedures
Part 2: 1994	Quality criteria and control of 35 mm silver gelatin microfilms
Part 3: 2001	Aperture card for 35 mm microfilm
Part 4: 1994	Microfilming of drawings of special and exceptional elongated sizes
Part 5: 1999	Test procedures for diazo duplicating of microfilm images in aperture cards
Part 6: 2000	Quality criteria and control of systems for enlargement from 35mm microfilm
BS ISO 6148:2001	Photography. Micrographic films, spools and cores. Dimensions
BS ISO 6196-4:1998	Micrographics. Vocabulary. Materials and packaging

BS ISO 6196-7:1992	Micrographics. Vocabulary. Computer micrographics
BS ISO 6198:1993	Micrographics. Readers for transparent microforms. Performance characteristics
BS ISO 6199:1991	Micrographics. Microfilming of documents on 16 mm and 35 mm silver-gelatin type microfilm. Operating procedures
BS ISO 6200:1999	Micrographics. First generation silver-gelatin microforms of source documents. Density specifications and method of measurement
BS ISO 7565:1993	Micrographics. Readers for transparent microforms. Measurement of characteristics
BS ISO 8126:2000	Micrographics. Duplicating film, silver, diazo and vesicular. Visual density. Specifications and measurement
BS ISO 8127-1:1989	Micrographics. A6 size microfilm jackets. Five-channel jacket for 16 mm microfilm
BS ISO 8127-2:1999	Micrographics. A6 size microfilm jackets. Other types of jacket for 16 mm and 35 mm microfilm
BS ISO 8514-1:2000	Micrographics. Alphanumeric computer output microforms. Quality control. Characteristics of the test slide and test data
BS ISO 8514-2:2000	Micrographics. Alphanumeric computer output microforms. Quality control. Method
BS ISO 9923:1994	Micrographics. Transparent A6 microfiche. Image arrangements
BS ISO 10197:1993	Micrographics. Reader-printers for transparent microforms
BS ISO 10198:1994	Micrographics. Rotary camera for 16 mm microfilm. Mechanical and optical characteristics
BS ISO 11928-1:2000	Micrographics. Quality control of graphic COM recorders. Characteristics of the test frames
BS ISO 11928-2:2000	Micrographics. Quality control of graphic COM recorders. Quality criteria and control
BS ISO 11962:2002	Micrographics. Image mark (blip) used with 16 mm and 35 mm roll microfilm
BS ISO/TR 12031:2000	Micrographics. Inspection of silver-gelatin microforms for evidence of deterioration

BS ISO 14648-1:2001	Micrographics. Quality control of COM recorders that generate images using a single internal display system. Characteristics of the software test target
BS ISO 14648-2:2001	Micrographics. Quality control of COM recorders that generate images using a single internal display system. Method of use
BS ISO 18905:2002	Imaging materials. Ammonia-processed diazo photographic film. Specifications for stability
BS ISO 18912:2002	Imaging materials. Processed vesicular photographic film. Specifications for stability
BS ISO 18919:1999	Photography. Thermally processed silver microfilm. Specifications for stability
BS EN 2484:1989	Specification for microfilming of drawings. Aperture card for 35 mm microfilm
BS EN 2499:1990	Specification for computer output microfiche (com) A6 microfiche
BS EN 2547:1989	Specification for filming of documents. Microfilm 105 mm (Microfiche A6)
BS EN 2575:1989	Specification for filming of documents. 16 mm microfilm

Storage

BS 4783	Storage, transportation and maintenance of media for use in data processing and information storage
Part 1: 1988	Recommendations for disk packs, storage modules and disk cartridges
Part 2: 1988	Recommendations for magnetic tape on open spools
Part 3: 1988	Recommendations for flexible disk cartridges
Part 4: 1988	Recommendations for magnetic tape cartridges and cassettes
Part 5: 1991	Recommendations for 12.7 mm magnetic tape cartridges for data interchange, recording at 1491 data bytes per millimetre on 18 tracks
Part 6: 1993	Recommendations for optical disk cartridges
Part 7: 1993	Recommendations for optical data disks
Part 8: 1994	Recommendations for 4mm and 8mm helical scan tape cartridges

BS 4783-5:1991	Storage, transportation and maintenance of media for use in data processing and information storage
BS 5454:2000	Recommendations for the storage and exhibition of archival documents
DISC PD 0024:2001	Archival documents. Guide to the interpretation of BS 5454:2000. Storage and exhibition of archival documents
BS ISO 18902:2001	Imaging materials. Processed photographic films, plates and papers. Filing enclosures and storage containers
BS ISO 18918:2000	Imaging materials. Processed photographic plates. Storage practices
BS EN 1047-2:2000	Secure storage units. Classification and methods of test for resistance to fire. Data rooms and data containers
BS-ISO 5466:1999	Storage of Processed Safety Photographic Film
BS-ISO 10356:1996	Storage and Handling of Nitrate-based motion picture film
BS-ISO 12606:1997	Care and preservation of magnetic audio recordings for motion picture and TV

Guidance on the management of electronic information is available from the Public Record Office; the following publications are particularly relevant:

- Management, Appraisal and Preservation of Electronic Records (2 vols, 1999);
- Good practice in managing electronic documents using Office 97 on a local area network (2000);
- Sustainable electronic records: strategies for the maintenance and preservation of electronic records and documents in the transition to 2004 (2001).

Appendix C: Model Retention and Disposal Schedule

XYZ GROUP – RETENTION AND DISPOSAL SCHEDULE

COMPANY SECRETARIAL DEPARTMENT   Ref: CoSec-3/2004
Annual Review to be completed by 30 September – Interim Review by 30 April

Doc Ref.	Document Description
	Board meetings
	Minute Books containing signed minutes (Note: a copy of the signed minutes is also scanned for permanent preservation as a computer file)
	Draft minutes and notes taken at meeting
	Agenda papers and notices (Note: An electronic copy of each agenda paper is also captured for permanent preservation as a computer file)
	Statutory registers held on head office server using Blueprint company secretarial software
	Register of members
	Register of directors and secretaries
	Register of directors' interests in shares and debentures
	Register of charges
	Register of substantial interests
	Files associated with statutory registers
CoSec/ChargeInstr	Copies of charge instruments
CoSec/DirShInt	Notifications of directors' share interests

Issued and approved by: .... on da▪

Reason	Retention period	Review action
Regulatory Evidence Paper.	Life of company.	
Business.	Minimum of 12 months.	To be reviewed by the Secretary at the Annual Interim Review and destroyed as confidential waste.
Evidence.	Life of the company but transferred to storage for permanent preservation after six years.	Transfer to storage to be approved by the Secretary at the Annual Review.
Regulatory Evidence.	Life of company.	
Regulatory.	Life of company.	
Regulatory.	Life of company.	
Regulatory.	Life of company.	
Regulatory.	Life of company.	
Regulatory.	Life of company.	
Business.	Eight months after the end of the financial year in which notification was made.	To be destroyed as standard waste after review by the Secretary or Deputy Secretary.

.... for implementation from ....

Appendix D: Examples of certificates

1 Certificate of authority

The records described below are records of [name of organisation] produced or acquired during the normal course of business. In accordance with its microfilming/ optical disk storage policy and procedures dated [. . . . . .], it is the normal business practice of [name of organisation] to [microfilm such records/store such records on optical disk].

The documents are copied with the specific intention of destroying the originals and retaining in their place permanent images in order to save time, space, filing equipment and to improve security. Destruction of the original documents is not to take place until the microfilm/optical disk copy has been checked for quality and completeness.

As the person responsible for the records described below, I hereby certify that I authorise [the microfilming of these records/copying of these records on to optical disk] and their subsequent destruction in accordance with the afore-mentioned policy and procedures.

List of Records

[In sufficient detail to ensure that the certificate can be related to the records on microfilm or optical disk]

Signed   Dated

(Position in organisation)

2 **Camera/computer operator's certificate**

I hereby certify that I have [microfilmed/copied by scanning on to optical disk] the documents listed above on roll/disk identification number [. . .] and to the best of my knowledge and belief the microform/information stored on each optical disk is a complete record of the documents passed to me for [micro-filming/scanning].

Signed   Dated

Camera/computer operator

3 Continuation certificate

I hereby certify that I have [filmed/copied by scanning on to optical disk] the material on roll/disk identification number [. . .] and that it is being continued on roll/disk identification number [. . .].

Signed   Dated

Camera operator

4 Certificate of acceptance

Category of record

Certificate of authority number

Microform/optical disk number

I hereby certify that the microforms/optical disks listed above, containing documents listed on the certificate of authority listed above have been checked by me and are of adequate quality and represent a true and accurate record of those documents.

Signed   Dated

(Position in organisation)

5 Certificate of destruction with list

I hereby certify that the documents listed below have been destroyed by me.

Signed   Dated

(Position in organisation)

[List of Records]

6 Certificate of destruction with list

I hereby certify that the documents listed on certificate of authority number [. . .] have been destroyed by me.

Signed   Dated

(Position in organisation)

Appendix E: Information survey form – records

INFORMATION SURVEY FORM – RECORDS

1. Record title	
2. Series/collection description	
3. Operational unit and location	
4. Purpose of records and reason for retention	
5. Current retention and review procedures	
6. Medium	
7. Location of records series/collection	
8. Arrangement of records	
9. Physical condition	
10. Date range	
11. Volume (in linear metres)	
12. Annual accumulation	
12. Active/inactive records	
13. Usage rate	
14. Duplication	
16. Documentation	
17. Restrictions on access and use	

Survey conducted by	Date of survey

Index

Accident book 184–185
Accounting records
  electronic, 85, 138–139
  Institute of Chartered Accountants
    statement, 140
  interim reports, 141, 148–149
  report and accounts, 140–141,
    148–149
  statutory retention requirements,
    113, 138–139, 148–149
Acknowledgement of claim by
  defendant
  postponement of limitation period,
    53–54
Advertising
  control, 197
Arthur Andersen 3–5, 250–251
Asbestos
  health and safety regulations,
    192–195
Asset registers, 214–215
Association for Information and
  Image Management, 252

Bankers' books
  as evidence, 33–34
Banking records 152–153
British Standards Institute (BSi), 252
  *Code of Practice for Information
    Security Management*, 93–94
  *Code of Practice for Legal
    Admissibility of Information
    Stored Electronically*, 11–12,
    86, 88, 89–93, 216

*Guide to the preparation of
  microfilm and other microforms
  that may be used in evidence,* 83
microfilm standards, 82, 83, 84,
  255–258
publications list, 254–259
standards on conditions for record
  storage, 84, 258–259
Buildings records, 206, 208–213
Business and Accounting Software
  Developers Association
  (BASDA)
VAT accounting software, 143
Business continuity
  security measures, 73–74
Business documents
  evidence, 30, 33
  hearsay evidence, 37, 82
  microfilm as evidence, 82

Certificates
  authority certificates, 262
  camera/computer operator, 262
  examples, 262–263
  retention periods, 43
Chemicals
  health and safety regulations,
    194–195
Civil proceedings
  disclosure of documents, 38–39
  hearsay evidence, 36–37, 82
  microfilm as evidence, 82
  proof of contents of documents,
    32–33

risk assessment of non-retention of evidence, 41–42

Companies
members' register, 112, 124–125
rectification orders, 115–116
registers, 102–104
retention of accounting records, 113, 138–139, 148–149
statutory retention requirements, 113
statutory returns, 104–105, 110–111

Companies Act 1985
statutory registers, 102, 103–104, 106–107
striking off of company, 98–99

Companies House
statutory returns, 104–105, 110–111

Company purchase of own shares
statutory requirement to retain contract, 113

Company records
on striking off, 98–99
on winding up, 97–98
share issue documentation retention period, 114–115, 124–125
statutory records, 102, 108–111

Company report and accounts
interim reports, 141, 148–149
retention, 140–141, 148–149

Computer output to microfilm (COM), 84

Consumer Credit Act 1974, 201

Consumer protection
Consumer Credit Act 1974, 201
product liability, 201–202
time limit for claims, 49
Unfair Terms in Consumer Contract Regulations 1999, 200

Continuation certificate, 263

Contracts
breach, 46–47
executed as a deed, 196, 204–205, 208–209
limitation periods, 196
tax records, 196
Unfair Contract Terms Act 1977, 200
Unfair Terms in Consumer Contract Regulations 1999, 200

CREST transactions, 112–113, 116

Criminal proceedings
hearsay evidence, 37–38, 82
microfilm as evidence, 82
proof of contents of documents, 31
risk assessment of non-retention of evidence, 42–43

Criminal records
employee, 155–156, 157

Cryptography, 95

Dangerous substances
health and safety regulations, 184–187
registers, 178

Data Protection Act 1998, 2, 19
conditions for processing personal data, 65–66
enforcement notices, 64–65
exemptions, 74
exemptions from notification requirements, 61–62
guidance on application to employment records, 74, 156–157
individual rights, 62–63
information management records, 217, 222–223
offences, 64–65
principles, 63–64, 65–74

requirements, 61–62
retention period of personal data, 2, 19, 70–71, 154, 217
sensitive personal data, 66–70
Data security
  controlling access to information, 72
  detecting breaches, 73–74
  ensuring business continuity, 73
  management, 72
  staff selection and training, 73
  transfer of records from one media to another, 78–79
Debenture holders register, 102, 106–107
Deeds
  contract executed as, 196, 204–205, 208–209
  limitation period, 206–207
  Deeds of covenant 152–153
Defamation
  Scottish limitation period for bringing an action, 59–60
  time limit for claims, 49
Deliberate concealment
  postponement of limitation period, 53
Direct marketing
  use of personal data, 75, 197
Directors
  register of interests, 102–103, 106–107, 131–133
Disability, claimant under
  postponement of limitation period, 53
Disclosure of documents
  civil proceedings, 38–39
Disposal instructions, 25–26
Disposal lists, 25
Disposal methods
  electronic records, 28

paper records, 27–28
Disposal policy
  benefits of applying, 5
  review, 24–25
  sensitivity categories, 26–27
  see also Retention policy
Dissolution
  company records, 97–98
Dividend records
  early disposal, 119–123
Dividends
  limitation periods for actions relating to, 123, 128–129
Documents
  as evidence, 29–39
  authentication of copy, 31
  central registry, 79–81
  civil proceedings, 32–33
  copies as evidence, 30, 33
  criminal proceedings, 31
  definition, 6–7, 76
  disclosure in civil proceedings, 38–39
  'in writing', 7
  original, 30–31
  proof of due execution, 34–35
  selection to become a record, 7
  stamped, 35–36
  see also Company records; Electronic records; Records
Documents under seal
  limitation period, 206–207
  register, 102–103, 106–107, 131–133
Donations to charitable and political organisations 152–153

Electronic document management (EDM), 86–87
Electronic records
  accounting records, 85, 138–139

British Standards Institute's Code
of Practice, 11–12, 86, 88,
89–94
certificates of deduction of tax, 146
certificates of tax credit, 146
disposal, 28
document and records
management systems, 86–88
for retention purposes, 85–86
health and safety, 181
media, 88–89
sensitive documents, 28, 156
software for specific records
retention purposes, 86
storage, 3, 88
tax, 145–146
use of personal data for direct
marketing, 75
VAT, 143
Electronic records management
(ERM), 87–88
Electronic signature, 35, 94–96
Employment records
guidance on application of the
Data Protection Act, 74,
156–157
health and safety, 180
Information Commission code, 154
PAYE and payroll, 147–149,
150–151, 162–165
pensions, 157–161, 166–177
recruitment records, 156–157,
160–161
retention periods, 154–156,
160–167
working time regulations, 154,
160–163
Enron Corp 3–5, 250–251
Evidence
bankers' books, 33–34
business documents, 30, 33
civil proceedings, 32–33
copies of documents, 30
criminal proceedings, 31
documentary, 29–39
electronic signature,
authentication by, 94
hearsay, 36–38, 82
microfilm records, 82–84
public documents, 34
risk assessment for civil actions,
41–42
Scottish law on admissibility of
documentary, 29

Financial services
money laundering regulations,
224–227, 244
record retention requirements,
224–249
'relevant business', 225–226
Financial Services Authority
Handbook, 226–249
Fire risk, 80
Fraudulent claim
postponement of limitation period,
53
Freedom of Information Act 2000
information management records,
217, 222–223

Gift aid forms 152–153

Health and Safety at Work Act 1974,
178–179
Health and safety records 42–43,
178–195
categories, 179
form of, 181
personal injury, 178
Hearsay
as evidence, 36–38, 82

civil proceedings, 36–37, 82
criminal proceedings, 37–38, 82
definition, 36

Incineration of paper documents, 28
Industrial injuries
  health and safety records, 180,
    184–185
Information Commission
  *The employment practices data
    protection code*, 154
Information management, 8–9
  Data Protection Act 1998, 217,
    222–223
  electronic, 87–88
  Freedom of Information Act 2000,
    217, 222–223
  records, 216–223
Information surveys
  example of form for records, 264
  records management, 21–23
  storage costs, 81
Inland Revenue *see* Tax records
Insolvency
  company records, 97–98
Institute of Chartered Secretaries and
  Administrators, 252
Insurance documents, 202–205
Intellectual property rights 209,
  212–213
Interest payments
  limitation periods for unclaimed,
    123, 128–129

Legacy
  time limit for claim for deceased
    person's personal estate, 50
Licences
  retention periods, 43
Limitation periods
  arbitration awards, 52

claim for deceased person's
  personal estate, 50
claim on a statute, 52
claim under the Consumer
  Protection Act 1987, 49
claim under the Fatal Accidents
  Act 1976, 48
claims for breach of contract,
  46–47
claims for breach of trust, 50
claims founded on tort, 47–50
contracts, 196
conversion of a chattel, 49–50
damages, 47–49, 207
deeds, 206–207
defamation action in Scotland,
  59–60
defamation claims, 49
dividend payments, actions
  relating to, 123, 128–129
documents under seal, 206–207
England and Wales, 43–46
equitable remedies, 52
evidence in legal proceedings,
  40–60
factors which postpone the
  running of time, 53–54
interest payments, unclaimed, 123,
  128–129
judgments, 52
Law Commission proposals for
  reform of limitation regime,
  54–56
libel, 49
malicious falsehood claims, 49
mortgages and charges claims,
  51–52
negligence claim, 48–49
personal injury action in Scotland,
  59
personal injury claims, 47–48, 180

recovery of land claim, 50–51
recovery of proceeds of sale of
    land, 51
rent recovery, 51
Scottish law, 56–60
Liquidation
company records, 97–98
Marketing records, 197, 204–205
Medical records
health and safety, 180, 184–185
Meetings
    retention of documentation,
    130–137
Microfilm records, 82
    as evidence, 82–84
    authentication, 83
    British and International
        Standards, 82, 83, 84, 255–258
Mistake, relief from consequences of
    postponement of limitation period,
    53
Money laundering
    record-keeping requirements for
        financial services, 224–225, 244

Paper documents, 7
    central registry, 79–81
    disposal methods, 27–28
    storage, 79–81
Part payment of claim by defendant
    postponement of limitation period,
    53–54
PAYE records 147–149, 150–151,
    162–165
Pension records 157–161, 166–177
Personal data
    Data Protection Act 1998, 2, 19,
        61–75, 154, 217
    guidance on application of the
        Data Protection Act to
        employment records, 74, 156–157

retention periods, 2, 19, 70–71,
    154
review, 71
security, 71–74
security implications of disposal,
    26–27
use for direct marketing, 75, 197
Personal injury
    health and safety records, 178
    Scottish limitation period for
        bringing an action, 59
    time limit for claims, 47–48, 180
    time limit for claims under the
        Consumer Protection Act 1987,
        49
Planning retention and disposal
    storage systems, 5–6
Prescription
    Scottish law, 56–60
Private companies
    retention of accounting records,
        113, 138, 148–149
Procedure manuals
    contents, 13
    see also Retention and disposal
        schedules
Product liability, 201–202
Project management
    retention policy, 13–14
Property records
    buildings records, 206, 208–213
    intellectual property rights, 209,
        212–213
    property assets, 214–215
    records centre, 207–208
Public companies
    retention of accounting records,
        113, 138, 148–149
Public documents
    as evidence, 34
Public Records Office (PRO), 253

Radioactive substances
  health and safety regulations,
    186–193
Records
  business needs, 20–21
  categories, 20
  central registry, 79–81
  choice of media, 76–79
  definition, 7
  freezing, 77–78
  life-cycle, 7
  risk assessment of non-retention,
    21
  sensitivity categories, 26–27
  storage conditions, 84
  see also Company records;
    Electronic records
Records management
  basic principles, 9
  electronic systems, 86–88
  external consultants, 14
  information surveys, 21–23, 264
  strategy, 11
  systems, 8–9
Records Management Society of
  Great Britain, 14, 252
Recruitment records
  *Employment Practices Data
    Protection Code*, 156–157
  retention, 156–157, 160–161
Rectification orders, 115–116
Recycling paper documents, 27
Registers
  allotments, 103
  CREST transactions, 112–113
  dangerous substances, 178
  debenture holders, 102, 106–107
  directors' interests, 102–103,
    106–107, 131–133
  form of, 103
  members, 112, 124–125

of documents sealed, 102–103,
    106–107, 131–133
  retention, 103–104
  statutory, 102, 103–104, 106–107
  transfers, 103
Retention and disposal schedules
  aims, 13
  categories of records, 20
  contents, 17–18
  disposal instructions, 25–26
  information surveys, 21–23, 264
  model schedule, 260–261
  property records, 208
  sensitivity categories, 26–27
Retention periods
  certificates, 43
  Data Protection Act 1998, 2, 19
  documentary evidence, 29
  exceptional circumstances, 19, 25
  factors influencing, 18–19
  health and safety records, 42–43,
    178–195
  impact of purposes for which
    records are kept, 19–20
  licences, 43
  personal data, 2, 19, 70–71, 154
  records of company in liquidation,
    97–98
  regulatory minimum, 19
  share transfer forms, 116–127
  storage media appropriate to, 79
  tables, 18–19
Retention policy
  aims and objectives, 10–13
  application, 15–16
  information surveys, 21–23,
    264
  monitoring, 16
  procedure manuals, 13
  project management, 13–14
  proportionate to needs, 14–15

review and update, 12, 16
sensitivity categories, 26–27
Review process
  disposal action, 24–25
  retention policies and schedules,
    12, 16
Rights issues 114–115
Risk assessment
  civil actions and non-retention of
    evidence, 41–42
  criminal actions, 42–43
  data security, 71
  non-retention of records, 21,
    41–42
  regulatory enforcement actions,
    42–43

Sale of Goods Act 1979, 199
Sale of Goods and Services Act 1982,
  199
Sales
  misleading prices, 198
  price indications, 198
  trade descriptions, 198
  Unsolicited Goods and Services
    Act 1971, 200
  weights and measures, 198
Sarbanes-Oxley Act
  retention of audit papers, 5
Scotland
  defamation limitation period,
    59–60
  documentary evidence, 29
  limitation, 56–60
  personal injury limitation period,
    59
  prescription, 56–60
Security
  British Standards Institute Code of
    Practice, 93–94
  personal data, 71–74

record disposal, 26–27
  see also Data security
Self assessment
  corporation tax records 144–145,
    150–151
  individuals' tax records 144–145,
    150–151
Sensitive documents
  disposal, 26–27, 156
  disposal of electronic records, 28,
    156
Sensitive personal data, 66–70, 156
Share issues
  documentation retention period,
    114–115, 124–125
Share registration
  CREST transactions, 112–113
  early disposal of records,
    119–123
  schedule of retention periods,
    124–129
Share transfers
  early disposal of forms, 119–123
  forged, 117–119
  paper document, 7
  retention of forms, 116–119,
    124–127
  stamped documents, 35–36
Shredding documents, 27
Signature
  electronic, 35, 94–96
  proof of validity, 35
Society of Archivists, 253
Software
  records retention purposes, 86
  statement of good practice for VAT
    accounting software, 142–143
Staff selection and training
  data security, 73
Stamp duty
  documents, 35–36

retrospective payment, 36
Stamped documents
    admissibility of document not
        properly stamped, 35–36
Storage
    British Standards Institute
        standards, 84, 258–259
    central registry, 79–81
    conditions, 84
    electronic records, 3, 88
    freezing a record, 77–78
    influence of business needs, 78
    media appropriate to retention
        period of records, 79
    microfilm, 82
    off-site, 80–81
    original documents and records, 77
    paper documents, 79–81
    records, 76–84
    reliability of transfer process, 78–79
    systems, 5–6
Storage costs
    accommodation costs, 81
    comparison, 81–82
    cost benefit, 78, 82
    electronic records, 3
    equipment costs, 81
    files and records, 2–3, 81–82
Striking off of company
    company records, 98–99

Tax records
    certificates of deduction of tax, 146
    certificates of tax credit, 146
    circumstances when records have to
        be kept for longer than usual,
        146–147
    contracts, 196
    corporation tax self assessment,
        144–145, 150–151
    form in which to be kept, 145–146
    Inland Revenue, 143–144
    PAYE and payroll records, 147–149,
        150–151, 162–165
    statutory retention requirements,
        113, 138
    value added tax, 141–143, 150–151
Time limits *see* Limitation periods

Unfair Contract Terms Act 1977, 200
Unfair Terms in Consumer Contract
    Regulations 1999, 200
Unsolicited Goods and Services Act
    1971, 200

Value added tax (VAT) records
    141–143, 150–151

Wills, 7
Winding up
    company records, 97–98